THE STORY

KANSAS STATE FOOTBALL:

The Greatest Turnaround in College Football History

Quality Sports Publications

Number *1.300* of 5,000
Limited Edition Copies

Bill Snyder

Dedication

To my own national champions:
Tammy, David Lee and Julie;
and in memory of everyone's favorite Wildcat,
Dev Nelson.

Dustjacket and title page design by Mick McCay
Dustjacket photo by Jeff Taylor
Title page photograph by Scott Irwig

All photographs compliments of:
Kansas State University Sports Information
Kansas State University Athletic Marketing
Kansas State University Photo Services
Wildcat Weekly
Jeff Taylor
George McCandless
Scott Irwig

Quality Sports Publications
10841 Hauser Court
Lenexa, Kansas 66210
(913) 469-1961
(800) 464-1116

Duane Brown, Project Coordinator
Melinda Brown, Designer
Mitch Holthus, Editorial Consultant
Scott Irwig, Photographic Editor

Printed in the U.S.A.
by
Walsworth Publishing Company

ISBN 1-885758-02-2

TABLE OF CONTENTS

FOREWORD   4

ACKNOWLEDGMENTS   5

INTRODUCTION   7

OVERVIEW   8
A PICTURE-PERFECT TURNAROUND

BILL SNYDER: 28
A PERFECT FIT

108   **1992:**
DEFENSE, SPECIAL TEAMS AND
A BLOCK PARTY

1989:   44
BABY STEPS OF PROGRESS

128   **1993:**
THE PROMISED LAND

1990:   64
THE 15-YARD OUT

152   **COPPER BOWL:**
TURNING COPPER INTO GOLD

1991:   86
CROSSING THE LINE

170   **CONCLUSION:**
A TOTAL COMMITMENT

*F*OREWORD

Americans love an underdog. We love sports stories that center on improbable victories, great upsets, overachievers and great turnarounds. We love movies like *Rudy* and *Hoosiers*. We adore hard-working teams who come from obscurity to win the big game. The 1980 USA hockey team is a great example, and so is the upset victory by the USA soccer team over Columbia in the 1994 World Cup.

Yet, those stories rarely happen in the real sports world and they seem to be even more rare in college football. It is almost a certainty that Notre Dame will pound Navy every year. The same case can be made for USC-Oregon State or Brigham Young over UTEP.

That is why the story of Kansas State's great football turnaround from 1989 to 1994 is certainly one of the best college football stories ever, and probably one of the best sports stories ever.

My first experience with K-State football was October 23, 1965. There were only 13,832 in attendance at old Memorial Stadium as K-State lost to Oklahoma, 27-0. Being an excited 8-year-old, I was naive and thought there were 113,832 in the crowd. Plus, I thought K-State was going to win every game.

However, I soon found out that it took a special devotion to love K-State football. It was devotion based on hope...hope for that big upset...hope for an occasional winning season...hope of eventual respect for the program.

That hope became reality on November 30, 1988. Following two "oh-for-autumn" seasons and with the overall program in serious jeopardy, K-State hired Bill Snyder as its head football coach. Snyder has centered his program on "hope" and "faith." Moreover, he demanded a full commitment from K-State's administration, students, faculty, alumni and fans.

It is a story that informs, inspires and entertains. It is a story that begins with a vision and ends with a bowl ring. It is a true story that starts with the "worst college football program" in America, according to *Sports Illustrated*. It is a true story that ends with the "most improved" program in America. It is the story of the "greatest turnaround in college football history."

Mitch Holthus
Voice of the Wildcats

ACKNOWLEDGEMENTS

Nobody these days is questioning the job done by Bill Snyder. We have called it the greatest turnaround in college football history. Because we live in a media-saturated society, that turnaround is no secret. But much of what happened, and how it happened, was untold. It was my wish to be able to tell that story.

An endeavor of this nature cannot be completed without the help of a lot of people. I have to start with Duane and Melinda Brown at Quality Sports Publications. I might have been able to write this, but you couldn't have read it because it wouldn't have been published. Melinda also designed the layout, which made your reading more lively. Scott Irwig, the chief photographer for QSP, helped me gather many of the breathtaking photos in this book. And we had fun doing it.

I want to thank Vern and Carol Osborne and Bob and Margaret Leonard for their hospitality during my research visits to Manhattan and their friendship over the years. I also owe a lot to Vern and Carol, more than I can say in this space. But without Vern's help, this book never would have happened.

Joan Friederich, Coach Snyder's wonderful secretary, put me in touch with the players featured in these pages. Her help was priceless. I also have a great secretary. She also happens to be my Mom (and it is hard to imagine a better one of either). She transcribed countless hours of interview tapes. Without her, *THE STORY* still would be in my mind. My Dad, the world's greatest proofreader, caught all my errors before you could.

Jeff Grantham of *Wildcat Weekly* supplied many of the photos you see in these pages and gave me some great tips on story angles. Thanks, Jeff. Thank you, too, to all the beat writers who filled the pages of my favorite newspapers with the accounts of the early days. You provided me with much of the background that made *THE STORY* worth reading. Since pictures are worth a thousand words, I owe about 200,000 thank yous to the photographers who captured the action.

Coach Snyder's staff is a big part of this story, and each member of that staff willingly shared with me his role in *THE STORY*. Ben Boyle and the staff in the K-State sports information office also deserve a lot of thanks. Erick Harper, who stood out on the gridiron in the '80s, now stands out in marketing the football team. I owe Erick and all his friends in the marketing department and the entire athletic department a big debt of gratitude.

Of course, without Coach Snyder and his players, this book would have been unnecessary. I enjoyed getting to know many of them and will be looking forward to building on those friendships.

And speaking of friendship, Mitch Holthus and I have been friends for more than six years. Our work together on this project has only enhanced the friendship. Mitch is an amazing person. His grasp of the intricacies of the Wildcats program is unparalleled, and his support and guidance were invaluable. No, check that. His support and guidance were a big, big, big, big, big help!

Finally, thank you to the fans of this program. Your support is a growing part of *THE STORY*. A little hint: as word gets out, be prepared for legions of others joining your numbers from all around the country.

Thank you for letting me into a part of your lives. I hope you enjoy this book half as much as I have enjoyed writing it. If you do, then I did my job.

David Smale

KANSAS STATE WILDCATS

Football Office
2201 Kimball Avenue
Manhattan, KS 66502-3398

Bill Snyder, Head Coach
913-532-5876
913-532-7956 (FAX)

INTRODUCTION

Dear Kansas State Fans:

When we came to Kansas State University, we knew we were accepting a great challenge. We knew about the difficulties that K-State had had, but we also knew that it was a challenge that could be met.

We knew we had the support of the university administration as well as that of the athletic department. And we also knew that we had the support of the outstanding fans of Kansas State. We had a lot to prove, but we knew that when we did, you would be there. We are grateful beyond words to those who have supported us from the beginning.

It was very special to step on the field at the Copper Bowl and hear the roar of the mostly Purple-clad crowd. We need that support.

It has been my pleasure to be associated with so many fine young men in our first five years at Kansas State. They have become very special to us and we consider it a privilege to have worked with them.

Similarly, we hope you have pleasure reading about how so many wonderful people have helped turn Kansas State football into a winning program.

Bill Snyder
Head Football Coach

8 Big Eight Conference

*O*VERVIEW:
A Picture-Perfect Turnaround

How do you take the worst program in the history of college football and make it respectable, even good? How do you take a team that has not won in 27 consecutive games and make it believe it can win every time it takes the field?

Those were just a couple of the questions facing Bill Snyder in 1989 as he prepared to become the 32nd man to coach the Kansas State Wildcats.

"First, we have to learn how not to beat ourselves," Snyder said shortly after being introduced as the head coach. "When we learn how to stop losing, then we have to learn how to win."

The Wildcat's Fourteen Goals for Success

UNITY -
Come together as never before.

BE TOUGH

GREAT EFFORT

NEVER GIVE UP

DON'T ACCEPT LOSING

EXPECT TO WIN

LEADERSHIP

IMPROVE -
Every day-as a player, person and student.

SELF DISCIPLINE -
Do it right, don't accept less.

ENTHUSIASM

ELIMINATE MISTAKES -
Don't beat yourself

NO SELF LIMITATIONS -
Expect more of yourself.

CONSISTENCY

RESPONSIBILITY

Sports Illustrated painted a pretty bleak picture of the Kansas State program in its college football preview issue in 1989. "When it comes to college football, nobody does it worse than Kansas State," Doug Looney wrote. "After 93 years of trying to play the game, the Wildcats' record is 299-509-41, dead last among the 106 schools in Division I-A." Looney also called the Wildcats "funny" to watch and revealed that the Cats were last in scoring offense and scoring defense nationally in the previous 43 years.

"I think you have to start with how bad is awful," Looney said recently. "Then it was worse than that. It certainly was way worse than horrific. It was hard for me to imagine how any collegiate football program could manage to get itself in that kind of shape. It reminded me a little bit of horse racing. It's just as hard to pick which horse is going to be last in a race as it is first. Kansas State achieved something monumental. They were the last horse in the race forever and ever."

That was the picture when Snyder arrived. Yet his first priority was not to win games. "We knew it was going to have to be a slow process, and part of it was just my

When Bill Snyder arrived, he knew that joyful celebrations were possible only if the Wildcats began to believe they could win, so he had The Wildcat's Fourteen Goals for Success mounted on the wall in the lockerroom.

belief that you need to build on a firm foundation," he said. "We wanted to bring high school youngsters in and develop them and keep them in our program over a period of time. We wanted them to understand the concept of trying to get better every single day of their lives.

"Consequently, if each one of them could do that over two, three, four or five years, then the bottom line was that they would come out at the other end a pretty good player, person and student. If we could do that collectively over that same extended period of time, we'd have a chance to be a good program made up of good players, good young people and good young students as well. Then our program would be on solid ground, and we wouldn't have as many ups and downs in the program."

His first day on the job, he told the press he thought he could be successful by caring enough not to settle for anything less than maximum effort. "It boils down to this," he said. "I'm not the best football coach in the United States, but what I'm going to do that maybe, maybe, is a little different, I'm really going to care. I'm going to care about the kids on this campus; I'm going to care about this campus. I'm going to care about the coaches.

"I'm going to make sure coaches that come in here lead a quality life; I'm going to make sure the student-athlete who comes in here leads a quality life. A lot of people work extremely hard, but maybe not as intelligently as they should. Therefore, the advancement is not quite as they like it or the results not quite as good as they'd like.

"I'm going to tell people that there is an administration here that

The Wildcats didn't win a lot of games in Snyder's first year, but it was not because of a lack of effort. Defensive intensity and hard work were Wildcats trademarks.

K-State has a supportive administration, including President Jon Wefald (right) with Mitch Holthus (upper) and Mr. K-State, Ernie Barrett (lower).

Carl Straw (opposite page) provided the toughness needed at the quarterback position.

will make sure we exist in some of the finest surroundings that exist in college football."

That last thought may be one of the reasons Snyder was able to accomplish the lofty goals set before him. Unlike many, if not all, of his predecessors, Snyder was backed, vocally and financially, by the administration, both in the athletic department and the university as a whole.

"We have been most fortunate to have an administration that is willing to allow this type of facility enhancement to take place," Snyder said of the more than $8 million in physical improvements in the football facilities that were completed by the beginning of his fifth season. "(KSU president) Dr. (Jon) Wefald, (vice president) Bob Krause, (former athletic directors) Steve Miller, Milt Richards and (current AD) Max Urick have been very supportive and active in the process.

"No one should overlook (director of development) Ernie Barrett when it comes to effort and dedication toward the cause. He has worked tirelessly and meant a great deal to this entire project."

Much of the improvements were committed before the money was raised. But Miller had promised to upgrade the facilities, and he was determined to fulfill his promise. "I've always had great trust in Steve," Snyder said. "He had to go out on a limb. I have a great deal of gratitude for Steve because he stuck by his word."

It started at the top. Wefald, the university president since 1986, embraced the new staff in the football office. After the *Sports Illustrated* article came out, he quickly contacted Looney with a challenge.

"He called me immediately and he said, 'I've got to tell you, of course, we didn't like that, but on the other hand it was absolutely true,'" Looney said. "He said, 'I'll tell you what, I want you to make me a promise that when we turn this thing around you'll come back and write about us again.' Of course, I couldn't make any promise on behalf of *Sports Illustrated*, but that was a safe one, because I knew Kansas State would never again win in the history of recorded man. So I said, 'Fine, Jon, that's a promise. You turn this thing around, and I'll be back.'

Once shackled with the Big Eight's worst football facilities, Kansas State now boasts a classy, complete lockerroom and weight room.

"Wefald just did a masterful job. Rather than just sending me off a sizzling letter accusing me of whatever he wanted to accuse me of, he approached that thing in an extremely positive way with no ill will to this day. I talked with him rather frequently on the phone. Actually Wefald had a great deal to do with it. He didn't just say, 'Don't ever come back to Manhattan, Kansas, because you haven't got any friends here.'"

Wefald's support was real. A great PR man for the university, he didn't merely pay lip service to the football program. "The things that were important were not all financial," Snyder said. "It was important in that it allowed me to realize that they had faith and trust in whatever I was all about."

What Snyder was all about was change, but not just for the sake of change. "What a lot of coaches do, which I think is a mistake, is they come in and they think that everything that was there before was bad," said Dana Dimel, an offensive line coach under Snyder, and a player and assistant coach in the previous three regimes. "The major problem is to come in and think that everything that somebody did before was wrong, and you've got to change everything. Coach didn't do that.

"What he did change were the expectations. I can remember as a graduate assistant, going into a game, and we didn't think about winning. You didn't expect to win. Now, when we go into games, we're shocked if we're behind."

Following the press conference to announce his hiring and a luncheon, he then met with the graduating seniors. Even though they no longer could contribute on the field, Snyder felt they could help in the turnaround. "I wanted a general response of what their feelings were," he said. "I knew that losing tamps down people. I was concerned as to how that would affect them. I wanted to know if there was anything that would help them. They were very active in that meeting. It allowed me to gain a lot of insight into what the returning players felt.

"They still were a part of the program. I want all the players to always feel that way."

The first training camp was a difficult one, especially because of the number of players available to Snyder and his staff. Only 47 scholarship players, 48 short of the maximum, were on campus, making a scout squad difficult to assemble. Through the season, many of those players were injured, meaning that often in practice, first teams had to square off against each other. But the effort paid off, ever-so-slightly, in that first season as the Wildcats garnered their first win since 1986.

Carl Straw engineered a thrilling, come-from-behind victory against North Texas with a 12-yard pass to Frank Hernandez on the game's final play. "I think that the reason we were able to hang on there and come back against North Texas is the fact that the coaches had instilled in us throughout the winter conditioning, through spring ball, and then through two-a-days, that we don't give up until the final bell sounds," said Erick Harper, who was a senior in Snyder's first year.

Bill Snyder looked at the Kansas State program with a microscope before making sweeping changes.

Although they didn't win another game that season, they were within a touchdown late in the fourth quarter in three more games.

The difference on the scoreboard really showed up the following season. The Wildcats won their first two games for the first time since 1982 and finished the non-conference season at 3-1. They ended their Division I-A losing streak and their Big Eight losing streak, both dating back to 1986. A revealing game was a 28-14 victory over Iowa State. The Cyclones led 14-7 at halftime in miserable conditions. There was a combination of rain and sleet, with a 15- to 20-mph wind that made the 44 degrees feel closer to 24.

While Iowa State failed to score after the intermission, the Cats scored 21 points, capitalizing on two Cyclones turnovers and a fake punt that misfired. "We had to try to build a crescendo of emotion," Snyder said following the game about the effort. "At this time of year, there's the tendency to drag. We needed an emotional ballgame and we expressed

15

The new Dev Nelson Press Box (previous page) towered over a capacity crowd for the Kansas game in 1993.

With the Cats' explosive offense in 1993, Willie the Wildcat (right) got some sore front legs from pushups.

Andre Coleman (opposite page) was one of five '93 seniors who signed with the NFL.

how important that it would be to play with emotion on every snap of the game."

The concept of improving each and every day meant great things for 1991. The 1990 season ended at 5-6. The Cats lost one game by giving up 21 points in the fourth quarter and another by just three points. A little bit of improvement meant "crossing the line" past respectability and into a winning record.

Mitch Holthus, the "Voice of the Wildcats," challenged the Cats to "cross the line" in a preseason meeting. The fruits of that speech meant the Purples would win on the road (twice), win more than they lost (a 7-4 record, including 4-3 in the Big Eight) and beat arch-rival Kansas (16-12 after trailing 12-3 in the fourth quarter).

"We went 5-6 my junior year and a lot of people around here were satisfied," said Michael Smith, reflecting on the fact that for the fans, five wins was a major accomplishment. "I don't think the guys on the football team and the coaching staff were really satisfied. When we won that seventh game, I think we crossed the line."

The winning record caught the nation's attention. Looney made good on his promise to Wefald and returned for a follow-up story for *Sports Illustrated*. He was impressed. "A miracle is occurring in Manhattan," he wrote. "This football program is downright acceptable....Seldom does a coach win by sheer force of personality. Snyder does. Guys like Bo Schembechler, Woody Hayes and Bear Bryant were all helped by their dominating personalities, but they were helped even more by superb players. Snyder is not blessed with the latter."

Even that started to change. "Look at the guys that K-State has in the pros," said Andre Coleman, a senior in 1993 who was drafted in the third round by the San Diego Chargers. "The '92 class had five guys go and this year we had another five. It started my freshman year. You could see the talent that K-State started bringing in. The coach-

The inside of the Dev Nelson Press Box has expansive room for the Wildcat Network team, as well as luxury boxes for comfortable viewing during inclement weather.

One of Bill Snyder's proudest moments occurred in 1992 when his son, Sean (opposite page), earned consensus all-America status as a punter.

es did a great job of recruiting to build a winning program."

The Wildcats' seven wins were the most since 1954 and set great expectations for the coming seasons. A lack of continuity on offense caused the Cats to fall back to 5-6 in 1992. But two things came out of that season that helped the 1993 Cats. The defense and special teams carried the team and won games when the offense really sputtered.

Even more important than that, the Cats averted a tailspin that could have set the program back several years. After a 3-0 start, K-State lost four straight games, three by large margins. But in a nationally televised game against Iowa State, the Cats blocked two punts, picked off three passes and claimed a 22-13 victory. It set the team back on course, a course that reaped big benefits in 1993.

"As hard as the 1992 season was to accept, in the years to come it will benefit tremendously this football program," Snyder said. "In fact, that truly was the case in

Michael Smith's acrobatic catches, like this one against Missouri in 1989, got the fans excited and gave a glimpse of the excitement to come.

1993. We had some fine young people in our program who remained competitive and dedicated throughout the '92 season. They were juniors, mostly, who had learned lessons about taking the little things for granted and would do everything they could not to allow the same things to happen in 1993."

As soon as the Cats arrived in Manhattan from their trip to Tokyo for a match-up with Nebraska, the preparation for 1993 began. A renewed enthusiasm for off-season workouts meant the majority of the returning players never left town. "What I saw was there were more people here over the summer working out on their own," Holthus said. "And that is a voluntary time. It was like calling for volunteers, and they were saying, 'Let's go to war,' instead of, 'We're going to take the summer off.' They were saying, 'We're going to make this happen.' And it's carried over. There are a lot of guys here this summer (1994)."

The Wildcats no longer are intimidated by any opponent, which has helped them build the best home record in the conference since 1990, much to the delight of the KSU Stadium crowd.

There were a lot of improbable finishes in 1993, if looked at from a distance. A 4-0 non-conference mark was highlighted by a victory at Minnesota in which the Cats jumped out early, blew the lead and then came back to win with a four-play goal-line stand in the final minute. The Cats lost their first game at Nebraska by 17, but trailed by only three points with less than eight minutes remaining.

They tied the 16th-ranked Colorado Buffaloes and then destroyed the 14th-ranked Oklahoma Sooners.

But the 9-2-1 record amassed by the Wildcats, the school's best in 84 years, was not a piece of luck. It was earned. Snyder and his staff put in dawn-to-dark hours, and then came back for more.

"People have great desires in life," Snyder said. "Mine was to succeed in this particular profession. I don't think it (his 16- to 18-hour workdays) is something that all of a sudden has happened. It fits the profession. It's a competitive profession and I quite obviously am competitive. There's the feeling that there's always more to do. Either you want to do it or you don't want to do it. If you don't want to do it, it's probably not the right profession for you to be in."

It's obviously the right profession for Snyder. After five seasons, including the Copper Bowl victory over Wyoming, Snyder's record is 27-28-1. The previous 56 games, the Wildcats were 6-48-2. That's an improvement of 20 games. Kansas State had won 27 games in its previous 118.

"I think you have to say it is (the greatest turnaround in college football history)," Looney said. "I think that the mood improved on the Kansas State campus because of this great turnaround.

"It's an inspiring chapter in collegiate sport. And I like to think that the turnaround was really done for the good of the entire university. That's how Wefald saw it. Now I'm sure that he had plenty of critics inside the house, but he just knew what the perception of having such a horrible football program (could do). It's sure easy for those who don't know to make the jump and say, 'All right, horrible football program, horrible university.' That's not fair, and that's not accurate, but nonetheless, that's what Kansas State was best known for – having a horrible football team.

"Now the fact that Bill Snyder turned it around so radically and so wonderfully and so expertly and so fast would spin anybody's head. That's a tribute certainly to Snyder. He can flat coach a football team."

He has earned Big Eight Coach of the Year three times in the last four years. He was named national Coach of the Year by ESPN in 1991 and was a finalist for the Football Writers Association of America Bear Bryant national coach of the year award and a semifinalist for the award given by both the Football News and the American Football Coaches Association in 1993.

He has led the Cats to a 21-2-1 home mark the past four years, second only to Nebraska. They own a 13-game home unbeaten string. The Cats have the fourth best overall record in the conference since 1990, including the best against non-conference opponents.

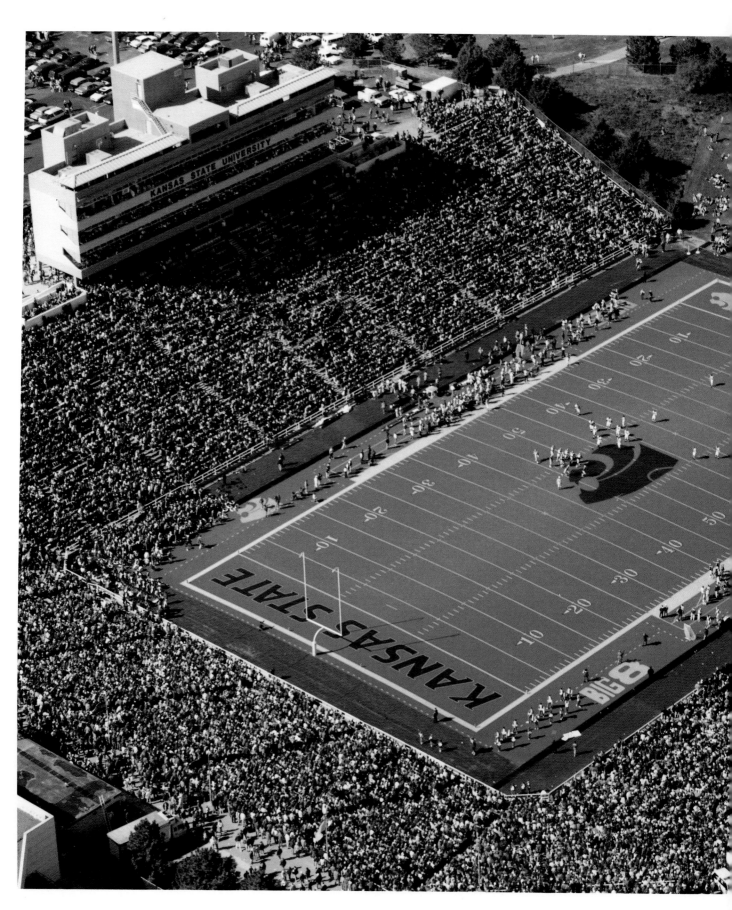

In 1993 alone, four different players were named to various all-America teams. Two K-Staters have been named consensus all-America in the past two years. Consider that only one other player in the 93-year history of the program had been so honored.

The Cats had the offensive and defensive Newcomers of the Year in 1993. The Wildcats also had 17 players honored as all-Big Eight, second best in the conference. The turnaround, though not complete, has no more doubters.

"We did have the greatest turnaround," Thomas Randolph said. "I think somewhere in some history book it should be documented as the greatest turnaround in college football history."

As the Cats continue to climb the national rankings, capacity crowds at KSU Stadium will become the rule rather than the exception.

BILL SNYDER
A PERFECT FIT

"Minor details are relative to a quarterback holding his fingers this far back from where they should be when he places his hands underneath the center and takes the snap, which constitutes the opportunity for a fumble, which constitutes the opportunity for a loss in a ballgame. Little things become big things very, very, very quickly, particularly when there are too many of them."

That quote, by Bill Snyder, pretty well summarizes his thinking and his meticulous attention to detail. At least it does according to no less an authority than Sean Snyder, 1992 consensus all-America punter at Kansas State, who also happens to be the head coach's oldest child.

"That's a very good summary," the younger Snyder said. "Nothing will get by him, as far as with Kansas State University, with football or with general athletics. He knows everybody who is working there, as far as secretaries, janitors or anybody who steps a foot in that building. Everything is detailed and he does most of it, if not all of it."

It's the kind of attention to detail that was necessary when Snyder took over the woeful Kansas State program in December 1988. In a program in which every detail seemed negative, Snyder set out to change it one detail at a time. It is a quality that is very apparent to everybody who meets him. And it is an inspiration to those who work for him.

"I look at it as being a young person in this profession and having the opportunity to learn from someone who has been in it a long time and has had a lot of success," said Bruce Van De Velde, an assistant athletic director/administrative assistant since 1992. "There's a commitment from Coach that we need to be concerned about the little things, because the little things add up to the big things."

When Snyder was hired away from the University of Iowa, where he had been the offensive coordinator for 10 years, in 1988, the KSU administration hardly could concern itself with anything bigger than getting a win. The Cats had not won a game in 2 1/2 seasons. It was then-athletic director Steve Miller's job to find somebody who could turn things around. He tried everything possible to go a different

When Steve Miller (seated, left) hired Bill Snyder, he found the man who fit Kansas State's recipe for success.

direction, but all the paths kept leading him back to Snyder.

"Ideally, what we wanted to do was find a Division I head coach," Miller said. "It was the top priority almost until the end. I was deeply aware of the fact that Kansas State required a particular kind of person. It needed a person who wasn't afraid to go out and see people. It needed a person who understood Kansas and the mentality of the people, because it is different from other states. It needed a person who wasn't afraid to start at the beginning."

That certainly fit Snyder. He had worked very slowly up the professional ladder, staying at each rung for extended periods. He had coached in high school, both as an assistant and a head coach, as a graduate assistant in college, then as an assistant in Division I-AA, before moving to Iowa.

Bill Snyder has earned his share of national honors, but husband and father are two titles he cherishes most.

"Nothing ever has been easy for me," Snyder said. "Nothing ever has been given to me. Nothing ever has come without great effort and a lot of hard work."

Miller put in a lot of hard work to find his head coach. "I interviewed 18 people in person," he said, "and I interviewed them in their hometowns. There was one guy in the process whom I really relied on and that was Jim Epps. Epps was my right-hand guy and he was the guy whom I ran things by. He also gave me a real objective point of view."

Miller had several coaches who fit his top criteria, but the fit just wasn't right. Much of the speculation early was that Memphis State head coach Charley Bailey was the front runner. Jack Bicknell of Boston College also was prominently mentioned. But Miller said that neither man made it all the way to his final list. Mike Price of Weber State also caught Miller's attention, but Miller kept coming back to Snyder. Although Snyder had no head coaching experience in Division I, or at any college for that matter, Miller said he knew Snyder was the one.

"When I met him in Iowa City, that was it," Miller said. "There was no turning me around at that point. He was the guy. And he was the guy because of these three reasons. One, he had been a high school coach and I liked the fact that he had come up through the ranks. Two, he was from St. Joseph (Missouri), so he knew the midwest.

"Finally, the two programs he was involved with had been in the dumper. He had helped turn around two programs.

"I tried not to hire him because I was afraid that I still had other opportunities for a

Division I-A head coach, but I just had a feeling. I've never been accused of letting facts stand in my way. I'm not afraid to be impulsive. I knew it was the right thing to do, and I did it."

On that visit, Miller and Chris Peterson, K-State's assistant athletic director for marketing who accompanied Miller, met with Snyder and his wife, Sharon. It was a conversation with Sharon, in fact, that may have sealed the decision. "She told us about the hours he put in," Miller said. "I knew that here was a guy who had 24 hours in a day and the worst he could do was tie you for the most hours spent. He was going to spend every minute that everybody else was and then go a minute longer, because he was going to do whatever it took."

That attention to detail paid its first dividend on September 30, 1989. North Texas, ironically one of the two colleges where Snyder and Hayden Fry previously had performed their turnaround, came to Manhattan as the top rated team in Division I-AA. The Wildcats fell behind with about a minute and a half left in the game. But the Wildcats marched down the field and won the game on the final play of the game on a play that was drawn up on the sideline by the players.

The maturity of Paul Watson into a star quarterback helped Snyder's Cats 'cross the line' in 1991.

31

Mitch Holthus, the "Voice of the Wildcats," says Snyder's attention to detail and the grilling of the plays into the players' minds enabled the sudden departure from the gameplan. "That tells you something about Coach Snyder," Holthus said. "Without him, they never would have gotten to that point. But once they got to that point, they said, 'We think we can run it; it will work.' Coach then had the ability as a coach to see the look in their eyes and say it's going to take a special play and they think they have it. Let them run it.

"It's a corny comparison, but in the movie *Hoosiers*, Gene Hackman turned his bas-

> Snyder values his coaches' opinions enough that he is in constant communication with them and he relays that advice to his players.

ketball team into one of discipline. They had to run 20 passes per possession every time, and whatever else it took to get that discipline. When they got to the state championship game at the last timeout, he wanted them to run a play they didn't want to run. They said, 'Coach, we can run the picket fence for Jimmy Chitwood.' He saw that look in their eyes and he said, 'Okay, let's run it.' That's the genius of a coach like Bill Snyder."

For a coach frequently called a genius, many people questioned the sanity of the decision to take over the Wildcats. "It's not one of the toughest jobs in the country; it's *the* toughest," Miller said at Snyder's hiring. It had been the graveyard for many of Snyder's predecessors. No coach has left Kansas State directly to another Division I head coaching job.

"Steve Miller had a lot to do with it," Snyder said of his decision. "Steve is a dynamic guy. He gave me an awfully strong impression that he was willing to make any and all commitments that were necessary to give the program a solid chance. I felt very comfortable with his support, and I felt he would certainly back up all the things that we had talked about that were important, things that would have to change, that were needed to be done here, to give the program a chance.

"I felt equal comfort with Dr. Wefald, and felt that he, too, truly was very supportive of the direction the program needed to go. I was impressed with the idea that he had an involvement in the program and an interest in helping it succeed. I think every president has an interest in their athletic program or their football program. What set Jon aside was that he had an interest in helping it succeed. He was willing to allow our program to flourish and do the things that needed to be done.

"Outside of that, maybe the rest of it slightly borders on the challenge, feeling like it could be done. Of course, having been an assistant, going to a head coaching position is always something that you're interested in doing. That was part of the reason to make the decision. And I guess the bottom line was, it was acceptable for my family. Everybody in my family was willing to run the risk."

Snyder also did not worry about the so-called experts who said Kansas State was a "black hole" and would swallow him, just like it had all the rest. "I didn't listen to those particular things," he said. "I don't know that there was anyone who had been in the same circumstance that I would be in. Nobody really knows unless they had been here."

Snyder's vitae is a lengthy one. He was a three-year letterwinner as a defensive back at William Jewell College in Liberty, Missouri. He held four coaching positions in the next five years, including one year as a graduate assistant at Southern California. His impact there varies, depending on to whom you listen. "I did absolutely nothing," he says. "I was a hanger-on. I didn't know how to be a graduate assistant. I was just there

33

and (head coach) John McKay didn't even know who I was. He would honor me with a word from time to time."

But Rod Humenuik, who was the offensive line coach at Southern Cal during Snyder's year there believes his new boss made more of an impression. Humenuik spent the past 24 years coaching in the pros with five different teams. He returned to college ball for the 1994 season for one reason. "Bill Snyder, period," he said. "I met him when he was at USC, and he's the reason I came here."

After the year at Southern California, Snyder spent the next seven years as a high school coach, compiling a 27-13-5 record. He then returned to the college ranks in 1974, where he has spent the last 20 years. He spent two years at Austin (Texas) College as the offensive coordinator and it was the last time he was involved with a program with a losing record (5-10-3). In 1976, he joined Fry at North Texas, where they led the Eagles to a 26-7 three-year record. Iowa's 10-year record during Snyder's tenure was 77-40-4. Consider this, the last time Iowa had a winning record before Fry and Snyder arrived was 1962.

"He was a grass-roots type of guy who felt you had to teach them how to play the game," said Manny Matsaikis, K-State's special teams coordinator and tight ends coach. Matsaikis was an assistant under Stan Parrish and was retained by Snyder. Three years ago, he left to become the offensive coordinator at Hofstra, but came back because of Snyder's approach. "The first thing Coach did was build a meeting room that was a teaching environment. My back-

ground is from a teaching standpoint. I got my teaching degree from here and I'm finishing my doctorate. I'm very comfortable with the way he does things from a teaching standpoint.

"You could tell he was an educator. Instead of going around in a fire engine and screaming how his offense was going to be, he was giving the coaches what they needed to teach."

Snyder sees his role, as a coach and a teacher, similar to

Andre Coleman (upper), Michael Smith (lower, pointing) and Kevin Lockett (opposite page) have benefitted from their exposure to Snyder's creative genius, and all three give the coach credit for their success.

that of a father. He has five children, three daughters and two sons. Besides Sean, who is 23, he has daughters Shannon (21) who is a student at Kansas State, Meredith (20), who lives in Greenville, Texas, and Whitney (8), who is in third grade. His other son, Ross, is a junior at Manhattan High School. He has tried to be there for his children and he tries to be there for his players.

"The opportunity is there all the time to counsel with a young person. It's not always problems. There are problem issues and there are just issues. Those present themselves on a very regular basis. We just talk on a very basic level, on a level that is goal oriented. How do we get from where we are to where we want to be."

Snyder's personal Christian faith also fits in there. He believes there is a correlation between his beliefs and his requirement that his players believe in the program. "It takes faith," he says. "Sometimes, in the beginning it's blind faith. But trust is a matter of faith. You believe in principles or you believe in a person, there's a reason that you have that faith."

Snyder's players pick up on that. "I learned a lot from Coach Snyder as far as being a player and a person," Andre Coleman said. "When you're a freshman, you try and avoid him. Guys are kind of intimidated by him. You see him and you turn and walk the other way. But when you start to mature, you see that he wants the best for you.

He's like a father. Guys just think he's being hard on you, but in reality, he's not. He's gearing you for the real world. I learned a lot from him and I've got the utmost respect for him."

That's a universal feeling for those who know Snyder. "What's important for me is I see how sincere he is in a profession that has been attacked for its insincerity, for its supposed abuse of players," Holthus said. "He is so refreshing because he is very sincere. He cares about these players. He genuinely cares about the people around him. I can see why his players fight their guts out for him."

One of those players is Michael Smith. Smith had just completed his freshman season, as a walk-on, when Snyder became the head coach. Smith was ready to return to his hometown of New Orleans and try to walk-on at Tulane, a

When Meredith Snyder was critically injured in an automobile accident, national wheelchair racer Kevin Saunders (left) provided her inspiration. He and Bruce Van De Velde enjoyed a moment together at the Copper Bowl.

school that had not given him a chance out of high school. Instead, Snyder offered him a scholarship and Smith went on to be the second leading receiver, in terms of yardage, in Big Eight Conference history. "Coach Snyder had a great deal to do with it," Smith said. "He developed a confidence in me to become a leader. I'm not the type of person to go screaming at somebody, but he told me I didn't have to lead that way, I could lead by example. I have carried that through the rest of my career and into the professional ranks."

Eric Gallon was another. Gallon gained 1,102 yards rushing as a junior in 1991. But in spring practice, he blew out his knee. The best-case scenario was a mid-season return. But Snyder pushed Gallon and helped him in his recovery so he could be back by the first game that fall. "My first impression as a freshman was, 'Oh, man, this guy doesn't care anything about us.' But as time went on, I realized we had something good. I think he deserves a lot of credit, more than people are giving him. He maybe should have been the national coach of the year, instead of just Big Eight Coach of the Year.

"He always liked to pass the credit, but if there was any blame, he liked to take all the blame. He said, 'If we lose the ball game, don't worry about it, it's on me.' That's the type of person he is, and that's the sign of a good person.

"When you become a man and you realize what type of man somebody is, you can depict whether he is a good man or a bad man. You learn these things as you get older, when you can know intrinsic values of a good man."

Snyder's work ethic inspires his players, as well as his assistant coaches. During the

Eric Gallon (1) credits Bill Snyder with enabling him to recover from a major knee injury.

summer, when many coaching staffs are taking vacations, honing their golf games, the Kansas State staff is in full force at the Vanier Football Complex. Jim Leavitt, co-defensive coordinator, was at the office at 7:30 p.m. on a Thursday night in June, looking for that little edge that might make a difference in September. "When you think about this, a lot of people wouldn't be doing this," he said. "Here I'm recruiting, finding another player here or there, looking at tape, trying to get ready to play somebody now. There are so many parts of the program, finding a player who can play, figuring out how to stop the

The Wildcats' 1993 coaching staff saw their labors pay off with a Copper Bowl victory.

counter that KU did against us last year and thinking about different things you can do with your position players to get them to play better."

It's just an extension of the head coach. "My dad lives and eats and breathes football," Sean Snyder said. "I believe that if anybody could turn this program around, it would be him because he is such a stickler for details. When it comes down to which way to vacuum the carpet, he's going to tell you."

That also helps Snyder run a clean program. With his hand in every detail of the program, he knows whether the rules are being followed. His reputation is impeccable. "In terms of self discipline, everybody has a definition of what all that means, and our approach within our program is virtually to 'do things right,'" Snyder said. "'Be where you're supposed to be, doing what you're supposed to be doing, when you're supposed to be doing it, and in the very best possible way it can be done.' That encompasses the players' approach to their school work, their approach to their personal lives, and it encompasses how they handle themselves as football athletes on the field."

It is that approach that brought many of Snyder's assistants to Manhattan. Del Miller, who arrived at Iowa a year before Snyder, came with him to K-State. He knew the status of the Wildcats program was not good, but he believed Snyder could change it. "We had a real commitment to give us a chance," Miller said. "But people make the difference. We've got great direction, great leadership with Coach Snyder."

There is no reason to believe that Snyder won't continue to build the program at Kansas State. He has the continued support of the administration. And he has the backing of the people. Brent Venables was a two-year player under Snyder, but he is a native of Salina, Kansas, and had grown up with the exposure to K-State's woes. He currently is a graduate assistant under Snyder.

"I played a good joke on some guys in my fraternity," he said. "I came in and said, 'Did you guys hear the news?' They said, 'No.' I said, 'I just came out of the staff meeting. Coach Snyder is resigning.' These guys are the biggest Coach Snyder-Kansas State fans, and they thought we were done. In this room there were about 10 guys, and everybody was quiet. Who were these guys? They're not associated with the football team. They're not football players. These are just college guys. They're having a good time in college, and they were truly very, very sad.

"I felt bad then. After about 15 minutes, I told them I was kidding, and they were mad. They were really mad. It wasn't going to make a big difference in their lives, one way or the other, but things like that make me realize how important he is to this program. He really means a whole lot to this community and to the state of Kansas, and it's just spreading."

It's spreading nationwide. Snyder has been named Big Eight Coach of the Year three times in the last four years. He was ESPN's national Coach of the Year in 1991 and was

Snyder is adamant about making sure the right people got credit for K-State's success.

a finalist for two national coaching honors following the 1993 season. But those honors are not what's important for this humble man. "There are a lot of people in this program who don't get all the attention that they deserve, and that's the unfortunate aspect of it. There's a lot of people a lot more deserving of having honors that they just don't give out than I am.

"Our assis-

tant coaches and the things that they do sometimes go unnoticed. When I went to Houston for the Bear Bryant award, nothing had assistant coaches' names on it. I went to Los Angeles for the one out there, there wasn't anything that had the assistant coaches on it. But it is, it is theirs, but it's hard to be in that position, just because they don't have an assistant coach of the year award, they don't have assistant staff of the year.

"But all of us know, it's no secret. You've got to have great people around you. If you don't have the kind of secretarial help that you need, if you don't have the kind of graduate assistants, if you don't have a great custodian, you won't have the kind of success you need. You have to look at those things. Our custodian keeps this building so kept-up

that a player comes in here and feels a special setting. Take the guy who is responsible for getting equipment on our players and taking good care of them in that respect. Players are sensitive to those kinds of things. You've got to have someone to be strong enough and disciplined enough and tough enough and yet compassionate enough, so you've got to be the same type of person as a coach would be.

Bill Snyder has earned the respect of his players, like Jaime Mendez, (opposite page) fellow coaches, like Kansas' Glen Mason (upper), and thousands of Wildcats fans.

Under Snyder's leadership, the Wildcats are staring down the future awaiting the next challenge.

We've got that downstairs."

Snyder also will not allow himself to get too satisfied with his accomplishments. He wants, and needs, to maintain his focus.

"I appreciate anybody's thoughts and respect them," he said. "But you can't afford to allow it to have an impact on what you do. I'm asked this all the time, 'Can you sit back and relax enough to appreciate what has taken place?' The history of this world is based on people who sat back and relaxed for a moment to do that.

"I don't want to say dynasty, because this is anything but a dynasty, but you've seen companies, countries and dynasties that have crumpled, because when they had reached a particular level, out of great effort on many people's parts, then human nature sets in and allows you to relax, to take an extra vacation, to get home a little bit earlier, and not to pay quite so much attention to certain details that you may have before. You take certain things for granted, assume that something will get done. Pretty soon all those little things add up, and now there's this downward spiral that can take place."

While some people may believe there are better coaches around the country, most people believe that there couldn't have been a better one for Kansas State. "He fits the socioeconomic environment here to deal with boosters, to deal with people at the univer-

sity," Holthus said. "He knows the value of this institution."

But Holthus also has a hard time believing there's a better coach anywhere. "I think he's the best coach anywhere," he said rather emphatically. "I'll put this guy up against Bill Walsh or Jimmy Johnson. If he has equal players in a vacuum, in an absolute-value situation, I'd put him up against anybody.

"I wasn't around for Chief Bender or Mike Ahearn or Pappy Waldorf or Charlie Bachman, but I can't imagine a better coach walking on this campus, or anywhere in college football. Somebody is going to have to prove to me that there's been a bigger turnaround or a greater story in college football than this one, and it deals with Bill Snyder. He walked in here and changed what was a moribund program into one that's nationally ranked. He means everything to that revival.

"There may come a day when Coach Snyder may leave this program. But the program now has a chance to survive because of him. He now has this program built to a point where someone could come in and take it over and keep it going. He has done to Kansas State what Bob Devaney did for Nebraska. He's done some things historically here that could last for a while."

Certainly, Snyder was a perfect fit for K-State. But when Holthus was asked if there was a better coach, not just for this program, but anywhere in football, he had a simple response.

"Find him."

1989

BABY STEPS OF PROGRESS

The first time Kansas State athletic director Steve Miller met Bill Snyder in 1988, he knew he was the man to take over the job of head football coach. He was impressed with Snyder's resume, of having worked his way through every step of coaching. He was impressed with the offense that Snyder ran at Iowa. And mostly, he was impressed with Snyder's tremendous organizational skills and attention to detail. But even Miller admits that he might not have been ready for the "get-after-it" approach of Snyder.

"I have to say that my impressions were understated when I first met him," Miller said. "After he came, I think that what I ended up doing was underestimating his focus and desire for detail. I thought that he was a regular human being; I thought he was like the rest of us. But I soon found out that he was not."

Things started happening right away.

"A part of the contract negotiations were that we would begin with the facilities right away," Snyder said. "The first things that we did were our players' lockerroom and meeting rooms." All of the facilities improvements were prioritized, with the top priority always being helping the players first. Snyder gives Miller all the credit for getting things done.

"Steve was very instrumental in making it happen," he said. "The money wasn't in

Wildcats like Erick Harper (below) were glad to see the arrival of Bill Snyder and his promises of physical improvements after pumping iron in a cramped weight room.

No longer did the Cats have to bail water to get to their lockers once the plush lockerroom was completed, including the stylish new logo in the carpet.

the pocket at the time, and that may have upset a few people. It was pretty easy at that time to look at the track record of Kansas State football and also see a football coach who hadn't done anything yet. There was an awful lot of money being spent, when there wasn't any money to be spent. There were 100 reasons not to spend the money and only one to spend it. Steve looked at it all and did it. Today, there probably isn't a soul who regrets that Steve did that."

But the construction hit a snag. While Miller and Snyder were at the Big Eight Conference meetings in Colorado Springs shortly after Snyder was hired, word came that the project had been stopped before it really got off the ground. The two men flew back to Manhattan, each with different ideas of how to get things back on track. While Miller tried to figure out how he could raise enough money, Snyder made an unusual offer.

"Even though Jack Vanier and I had had a meeting when I had hired Bill and Jack had guaranteed that he would support me if I needed it," Miller recalled, "I didn't want to go to Jack that early in the process. We came back from the Big Eight meetings and Bill came in to see me. He said, 'I'll give you a check for $100,000.' I said, 'What?' He said, 'I'll give you $100,000 of my own money. I'll write you a check so we can get this thing started. Let's dig a hole. Let's put a brick up. Let's show the kids that we're going to do this, because we're recruiting off the idea that we're going to make some significant changes.'

"At that moment, it became very apparent to me that this guy was different. While I was serious and I knew he was serious, I don't think I realized how serious he was until that moment."

Miller did not take Snyder's money, but armed with that commitment from the head coach, he was able to raise enough to finish the first-year improvements. The Vanier

Football Complex is proof of that.

Though Snyder says he was serious about his offer, he was glad Miller didn't accept it. "I'm not real sure where I was going to get the money," he jokes. "I knew that I would have to cash in a few chips along the way in order to do that, but I would have been able to put it together. There was a way. I just didn't have $100,000 laying around."

Snyder is a private man, so very few people knew about his and Miller's conversation. But the right people knew. "I wouldn't have accepted it," Miller said. "But it was at that moment that I realized that my efforts, while I thought they were good at the time, were not good enough. I just simply said, 'That's it, I'm going to get this done no matter what.' I guess what he said was, 'Steve, we both said we would do this. I'm going to do whatever I have to do to do this. What are you going to do?'"

Not all the cosmetic changes were buildings, either. Snyder believed the team needed to get rid of its passive attitude and one place to start was in the clothes they were wearing. Snyder contracted with Tom Bookwalter of Manhattan to design a new logo and corresponding uniforms. Bookwalter worked with the company that designed Iowa's progressive logo when Snyder and Hayden Fry arrived in Iowa City.

The athletic department called a showing for representatives from various parts of the campus to view Bookwalter's first ideas, which met with mixed reviews. Snyder later invited Bookwalter to his office. "We didn't want a passive logo," Snyder said. "We wanted it to be unique; we wanted it to be something that didn't have to say Kansas State. It needed to say it by itself. I wanted that one dynamic logo that looked different from anything else you had ever seen and would make you say, 'That's Kansas State.'"

Bookwalter came back with three similar designs. Besides the one chosen, one other had the final design with a white border around it and the third had a few more edges. The new Kansas State logo now is emblazoned on

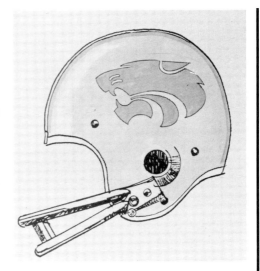

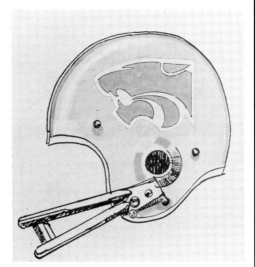

Tom Bookwalter developed several ideas for a new logo, but none met Snyder's approval. He came back with three more choices, from which Snyder and his players chose the symbol (lower) that now can be seen throughout the state and region.

Eric Wolford and the PowerCats have raised Kansas State from bashful kittens to furious Wildcats.

license plates and T-shirts all across the country, all without having to say Kansas State. Snyder had his wish...the logo had its effect.

New facilities are nice, and fancy uniforms may make the players feel more appreciated, but Snyder knew that his mission would be destined for failure if he left out one thing.

Work. Plenty of it.

Beginning with his first spring practice, the holdovers knew things were different. "He works you hard," said Michael Smith, a red-shirt sophomore when Snyder began at Kansas State. "He's going to push you until you figure you can't go any more, and then you're going to find that second wind to go on."

Not everybody liked it, though. "We lost (a few) guys right off the bat," said Frank Hernandez, who was a true sophomore that season. "A lot of it had to do with the work

Erick Harper has seen it all. He came to Kansas State as a freshman full of confidence and enthusiasm. Three years later, he had been a part of only two Kansas State victories and his enthusiasm was greatly dampened. But even though Kansas State had received national notoriety in *Sports Illustrated* as the worst program in college football, Harper was determined to stick it out.

"When I signed a scholarship to come here, my dad told me, 'You made the bed, you sleep in it 'til it's all said and done.' So there was no chance of me going anywhere else." But as Harper prepared for his senior year, Bill Snyder arrived as the 32nd coach in Kansas State history. There was hope that maybe Snyder was the man who could turn around the program.

He was.

For the past four years as a member of the K-State department of athletics, Harper has seen how it was done. He's not surprised. "You could see in Coach Snyder that he had a presence about him, a sense of confidence that he instilled in us right from the start that he could get it done," Harper recalled. "We just believed what he said.

"His main focus was that he was going to give us a chance to win in the fourth quarter. I had played against his offensive system for two years when we played Iowa. I saw the system working. We weren't able to compete for four full quarters with those teams. We could compete for three, three and a half quarters, but when it got to the fourth, we were small in numbers and we just kind of wore down.

"Coach Snyder and his staff instilled the fact that we don't give up until the final bell sounds. It all became a mental thing. They never let us settle for just getting by. When you get to a point where you can close it out, stick a nail in the coffin and get it done."

While Harper was watching Snyder's offense work at Iowa, he was being watched by Snyder. He was the one player whom the Iowa offense prepared for the week before the game. "He was a very good player," Snyder said. "When we got here, we anticipated that Erick was going to be a real fine player for us."

Harper has gone on to become a fine support person for the Wildcats. As the assistant director of marketing, his job is to promote the Wildcats, a much easier job now that the Cats are winning. He is the director of the Golden Cats, a group of former players, coaches, managers and trainers who raise money for the football program. Just like Snyder's success does not surprise Harper, Harper's success

ethic that Coach Snyder instilled right away into the program. Not degrading the work ethic that was there before, but the one that he brought in was a lot more demanding. The time restraints were greater.

"I think the guys who left had gotten used to a different style and they were not willing to adjust. That's all it was, an adjustment, but it was a worthy one, of course. A lot of guys dropped out because of the drastic change. It's like a drop in temperature. It kind of shocked everyone. Either you made it through that shock or you fell by the way-side."

Thomas Randolph signed with Kansas State after Snyder arrived, but as a senior at Manhattan High School, he got a first-hand look at the difference in attitude. It is what convinced him to come to Kansas State even though most of his friends and his high school coaches were saying it was a bad choice.

"My senior year (before Snyder arrived), I went to watch the Oklahoma State game, and I was at practice the week before," Randolph said. "That was my recruiting trip. One day it started raining and they just left the field. *Thirty minutes of practice and they left the field!* I couldn't believe that. In high school, the lightning has to be hitting the field for us to leave the field. And then we might have moved to the other end of the field.

"When spring ball came around and I saw how they were practicing, I knew then that Coach Snyder was for real."

Of course, nobody on the outside knew how practices were going. In order to "avoid as many distractions as we possibly can and put our players in the best possible

does not surprise his coach.

"He was a guy who really had his feet on the ground," Snyder said. "He was very level-headed about everything that went on, a good, solid individual. During that year he was here with us, he tried to be a very positive leader in his own right. We would have loved to have had him for a longer period of time."

Harper's highlight as a player was the victory against North Texas. He had experienced all 30 games of the winless streak, and this looked to be his last chance to celebrate a win. But that's not the only reason he enjoyed it so much.

"I probably wanted that game worse than any game in my career," he said. "Coming out of high school in Texas, a coach at North Texas who was recruiting me told me in a nutshell that it would be great if I signed with a big-time school in February, but where

would I be in two years. I have no idea where that coach is now and I couldn't remember his name or his face if I saw it today. But I wanted that game to prove to that coach that even four years later, I still was doing well."

He didn't get the chance to say it to the coach in person, but he had proved coming to Kansas State was the right choice. He also believes it is pretty obvious that Bill Snyder was the right choice for Kansas State. "I'm just as happy as those guys are right now with the success that they have had," he said. "I played with some of those guys who

just finished. They just got (in with) Snyder from the ground floor."

A floor laid with players like Harper as the foundation.

Frank Hernandez (83) and Michael Smith became best friends as well as one of the top receiving tandems in Big Eight history.

learning environment that we can," Snyder closed practices. And the dressing room. And the open line into his office. And...

The media hated it. Reporters complained that they needed to have access to the players, assistant coaches, trainers, and the like to do their job properly. They missed the opportunity to call the coach and chat about the previous week's game when they were in the mood to write. They saw it as a personal slap, even though Snyder denied that it had anything to do with them. "We had a lot of people who would like to be there watching us practice, and I would have liked for them to be in there," he said. "I enjoyed having people there and being able to visit with the people about our team and our players. But it was imperative for us to remain focused and work as hard as we could to avoid disrupting the players' concentration."

After what seemed like years of work leading up to the opener, Snyder's Cats arrived in Tempe, Arizona, for a mismatch with the Arizona State Sun Devils. Against one of the Pac-10's better teams, the short-handed Wildcats got shut out. But the 31-0 score was not entirely indicative of the effort put out by the Cats.

William Price picked off Paul Justin's pass on ASU's first play from scrimmage and the Cats drove down to the Arizona State 9-yard line. But a David Kruger field goal attempt was wide right. With a 31-point difference, it's hard to imagine that a missed three-pointer could have a dramatic effect on the outcome, but Snyder is quite sure that his team lost a little enthusiasm with the missed opportunity.

"I think we let down a little bit," Snyder said. "But then that's part of the learning process."

Once Arizona State got into the game, however, it hardly was a game. Justin rebounded from the interception to pick apart the KSU defense. His TD pass to Ryan McReynolds made the score 14-0 in the first quarter, and the Devils coasted. They outgained the Wildcats, 431 yards to 107, and had 23 first downs to the Cats' eight.

If the Cats went into the game with a short stick, they came out with a twig. The Cats had only 63 scholarship players (the maximum was 95) on the squad to begin with, and during the preseason, others went down. Starting offensive linemen Eric Zabelin and Will McCain missed the game with injuries. Starting linebackers Brooks Barta and

James Enin-Okut did not start, though both later played.

Starting quarterback Carl Straw twisted his ankle in the fourth quarter and left the stadium on crutches, the same assistance used by linebacker Jeff Lowe, who was lost for the season with a knee injury. Nose guard Anthony Williams hobbled off the field as well.

"You go with what you've got," Snyder said. "You can't spend the time worrying about things that already have taken place or things that you don't have control over. We just had to focus on those guys who were still on the field and were still capable of playing, and do what you can with the ones that you have.

"The experience of the Arizona State game was simply, 'How much does all this mean to you? Is it important enough that it hurts, that it pains you to lose?'"

The injury to Straw put the pressure on sophomore Paul Watson. Watson had arrived on campus as one of the most highly touted players in the program's history. But injuries had limited him to seven quarters of action in his first two years (one was a redshirt year) at Kansas State. He would receive the starting nod in one of the most disappointing games in Snyder's coaching career.

The Northern Iowa Panthers came to Manhattan for Snyder's home debut fresh off a 22-14 loss to Mankato State. The Panthers were a Division I-AA team who resided in Cedar Falls, Iowa, about 75 miles from Iowa City, where Snyder had spent the previous 10 years establishing his coaching reputation with the Division I-power Iowa Hawkeyes.

Snyder refrained from calling the game a "must-win," and he was very glad afterward that he had. "I'm glad I didn't say this was the most important game that we would ever play, but it was a (terrible) loss," he said. "There are a lot of players and coaches down there (in the lockerroom) who hurt really bad."

None hurt more than Snyder. "Maybe there was a little bit to do with the fact that I had come from Iowa and certainly didn't want to lose to an Iowa school, but I think there was a dose of reality in there as well," he said. "A lot of people could write off the Arizona State ballgame, because it was Arizona State. It was a name program at the time. Northern Iowa wasn't the case. But Northern Iowa was an extremely good football

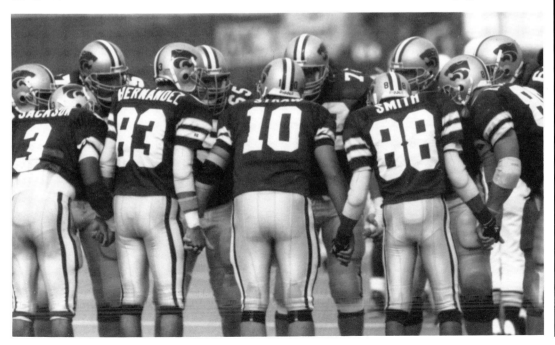

Team unity is Goal No. 1 of The Wildcat's Fourteen Goals for Success.

team."

The game was as winable as any the Cats had played in the 29-game winless streak. The previous two encounters with Northern Iowa were played when the Panthers were one of Division I-AA's elite teams. The Wildcats had their new uniforms and a new positive attitude. "We've invested more time, more energy, more hours on the field, more hours watching tape than we ever have," fifth-year senior Chad Faulkner said. "(The pregame attitude) was high, real high."

Even the crowd of 28,275 expected a win.

The game itself was one of frustration...and hope. The Wildcats took 27 plays from scrimmage in the first half and generated only 60 yards of offense. Northern Iowa managed only 84 yards on 30 plays in the first half. While Northern Iowa finally got going in the third quarter, scoring on a Ken Macklin-to-Brian Mitchell 36-yard pass, Kansas State

With all the accolades Frank Hernandez received – second-team all-conference his junior year, third all-time K-State leader in pass receptions, fourth all-time in yardage – he surely will be most remembered for one play.

The Catch.

September 30, 1989. North Texas 17, Kansas State 14. Four seconds left. KSU ball on the North Texas 12. All Hernandez did was drive his defender several yards deep in the end zone, cut back to the front left corner and snare Carl Straw's pass for the game-winning points. All that did was break a 30-game winless streak and send 26,564 into utter frenzy.

"I've caught a lot of touchdowns in my career, even in high school, but none have had such an impact on my life," Hernandez said. "I came home and it was all over the news. It was the CNN Play of the Day. Everybody was going nuts. It didn't really hit me until the next day when we saw the

papers."

However, the play didn't have a name. It was more of a "You run to the blue Ford past the manhole cover and cut back, and I'll hit you."

Straw said the hours of preparation allowed the final play to work. "Frank just ran a deep out in the end zone," he said. "We watched so many films that week, I knew he was going to be open because that guy dropped so deep.

"Frank was supposed to go 10 yards, he went 14. I was supposed to take a three-step drop, I took a five-step drop. So it was a miracle, but it worked."

The play may not have been run perfectly, but the celebration certainly was. "I couldn't breath," Hernandez said. "It was so hot, but yet I was so happy. I wanted to do cartwheels and

continued to falter.

The Cats had a 32-yard field goal blocked, and missed fourth-and-one opportunities at their own 28 and the UNI 26.

But then came the hope. Chris Cobb came in for the injured Watson – a neck injury sent him to the hospital – and engineered a 62-yard drive for a touchdown pass to Frank Hernandez with 55 seconds left. The Cats went for two – with an eye on the victory – and con-

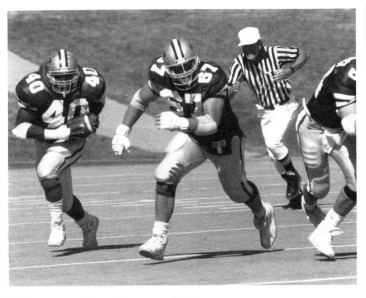

Bill Snyder's pass-oriented offense still allowed for the power sweep.

verted with Cobb throwing to Al Jones, making the score 10-8.

Although Northern Iowa recovered the on-side kick, sealing the Wildcats' loss, Snyder was pleased with the effort. "Nobody gave up on the sidelines," he said. "Nobody gave up on our offense. Nobody gave up on our defense. The kids kept coming back and I'm proud of them."

But following the game was one of the most painful experiences in Snyder's coach-

jump in all the excitement, but I couldn't. Mike (Smith) came over there, and all the people came and we just got swarmed in a matter of seconds.

"The next thing I know, Mike is on the ground, and he's reaching up. I'm trying to pull him up, and I'm just exhausted. We could not breathe. I thought I was going to suffocate. We just dragged ourselves up the hill to the lockerroom, and it was like a dream."

The finish may have been dream-like, but it was a confident team that marched downfield. "That was the first game that everybody believed in those 14 goals, especially the one about never giving up," Smith said. That confidence was remarkable, considering how the Cats had fallen behind.

They had played a good game defensively against the No. 1-ranked Eagles from Division I-AA. With less than two minutes remaining, North Texas was staring at fourth-and-19 at the Wildcats 47. Only the Cats' history could beat them now. History dressed

up as a fluke play as a Hail Mary pass was caught in the end zone for the North Texas lead.

"We were thinking, 'This place is cursed,'" Hernandez said. "'There is no way this is happening to us. We're playing the game of our lives here and we're losing at the last possible minute.' We were just so depressed. Then we started getting it together. Mike made some fantastic catches along the way to get us down there. They were all along the sidelines, from one sideline to the other."

That set up Hernandez for the final play. While most thought it would go to Smith, because he had made several of the catches on the final drive, to Hernandez and Smith it hardly mattered. They not only were the first junior receivers in Big Eight history both to surpass 1,000 career receiving yards, they did it while developing a deep friendship. They roomed together for four years and stay close three years after completing their col-

legiate careers.

"He will be the best man at my wedding," Smith said of Hernandez. "I miss him. We've both gone our separate ways. We still keep in touch, and there's nothing in the world I would trade for that friendship."

Snyder feels the friendship helped both players. "They did everything together," he said. "They competed together. Frank would try hard to compete as hard as Michael did. They were kind of entwined. Because of that, Frank got quite a bit of notoriety."

Nothing like what he got after "The Catch."

ing career. As he walked off the field, he met the television cameras. "It was a night ballgame so it was about 10:00 or 10:30 when we had the interview," he said. "That was difficult. Those were hard questions to have to answer, and to do it right at the end of the ballgame was painful."

Another loss to Northern Illinois left the Wildcats with only one more chance to break the streak before the Big Eight season and a journey into 19-straight-winless

games territory. And strange as it sounds, from top to bottom the Wildcats went into their fourth game with a positive attitude.

"That was the thing that we were fighting all the time," Snyder said. "We've got to have an attitude that we can win. We've got to have confidence going into any ballgame that we've got an excellent chance to win if we do this, this, and this, and do them well. Our players were pretty good about that because they did respond and they did believe.

"I'm sure there were moments when that belief was a fault line to an earthquake, but they did believe."

It paid off.

Culminating in a drive that would be relived five seasons later against Oklahoma State, the Wildcats earned their nickname with a last-second 20-17 victory over North Texas. It ended a 30-game winless streak that extended back to when most of the Wildcats were in high school. And for once, the Cats found a way to win a game that should have been lost, instead of the other way around.

Mitch Holthus, the Voice of the Wildcats, sat in the pressbox with "powder burns, because I was here doing the play-by-play of the Austin Peay game in 1987," he said. "I was here doing the play-by-play of the game they gave away to Iowa State in 1987, the games they gave away to Louisiana Tech and Tulane in 1988. I've got probably the same powder burns that some of those juniors and seniors had on that team of like, 'Here we go again.' So, yes, I was in utter amazement to see them pull it out in the way they did." As the drive unfolded, he gradually started to believe that this could be the game that broke the streak. Here is his call of the final play on the 10-play, 85-yard drive in the final 1:31.

"Smith is in the slot left, Hernandez the split end left. Flanker right is (Patrick) Jackson. The quarterback is Straw. He takes the snap, back to throw, North Texas rushing. Near-side pass to Hernandez! He got it! He got it! He got it! Touchdown! Touchdown! Touchdown K-State! K-State wins! K-State wins! Touchdown on the final play of the game to Hernandez! What it is, what it is, it's a big, big, big, big, big, big touchdown!"

Most observers thought the game would go down as No. 31 without a win. On fourth-and-19 from the Cats 47 with less than two minutes remaining, North Texas' Carl Brewer caught a Hail Mary pass for a touchdown to give the Eagles a 17-14 lead.

"It was tough, because you sit there and you say, 'Here we go again,'" senior Erick Harper recalled. "But at the same time, you say, 'Maybe it's time for our luck to change. Lady Luck is shining on us this day. We need this.' Then you get to the point where you say, 'It's going to happen. We're going to get it done.' I had confidence in the offense."

After Frank Hernandez snared Carl Straw's last-second pass to defeat North Texas (opposite page), he celebrated with buddy Michael Smith while the crowd was busy hugging the goal posts.

Since his arrival, Snyder had been teaching patience and perseverance. If there ever was a time to practice what he preached, this was it.

"I think the guys went out there and said, 'We can still win this game. If there is one second on the clock, we still can win this game,'" Michael Smith said. "We went out and did it. It was great for the program."

Actually, that one second was more than remained when the winning points were scored. Straw connected to Smith four times for 77 yards in the drive that left the Cats with a third-and-10 at the North Texas 12-yard line with four seconds left. The touchdown pass to Hernandez wasn't even a play in the Kansas State playbook. "It was sort of a made-up call," Hernandez said. "Carl told Coach that it would be wide open and it worked perfectly."

Bedlam followed as the goal posts were torn down and the field was a sea of delirious fans. Most of the players never had experienced a college win and most didn't know how to react. "The last thing I knew was when I threw it, I got hit," Straw said. "I laid on my back and all of a sudden this roar came out. I thought he must have caught it. It wasn't but a couple of seconds later I was pounced on by fans. It was unbelievable."

Something else came out of the victory against North Texas – confidence. The Wildcats bought into Snyder's never-say-quit attitude and with the late-game heroics, every one of the Cats believed they had a chance to beat Nebraska the following week in Lincoln. But the Cats not only were fighting the No. 3-ranked Huskers, they were fighting history. They had not beaten Nebraska since 1968 and they stood 10-61-2 all-time against Big Red.

To compound things, the Cats went into the game with NU with about half the number of scholarship players allowable.

Welcome to Reality Check 101. The Huskers pasted

Michael Smith was ready to stay home. Not that he had a lot of promise if he stayed in New Orleans, sportswise. There just didn't seem to be much future for him in Manhattan, Kansas.

Fortunately for Kansas State fans, Smith's parents advised him to give this new guy a chance. After all, "Why would you want to go somewhere that didn't want you in the first place?" they asked. So Smith returned to Kansas State for his sophomore season.

When he finally left, he was the most decorated receiver in Kansas State history.

Smith is the second leading receiver in Big Eight history, in terms of yardage. He is the K-State career leader in receptions (179), yards receiving (2,457), 100-yard receiving games (nine) and touchdown receptions (11). He also holds season and game records for receptions and is tied with John Williams as the leader with three touchdowns in a game. Oh yeah, he also holds the career mark for smiles.

"Michael is an awfully good youngster," Bill Snyder said. "He really liked to play the game. He had fun with it." It wasn't always that way.

As a senior at Jesuit High School in New Orleans, he was not highly recruited. In fact, Tulane University, located in New Orleans only offered him the opportunity to walk on.

the Cats, 58-7, gaining 542 yards on the ground and 723 yards of total offense. But the Wildcats were not destroyed. "I told the players we just got our fannies whacked," Snyder said after the game. "I told them they had two directions to go and it was up to them to decide which way.

"I won't give up on these players. I don't want them to think winning can't happen."

Holthus, who suffered through the years of losing every game, saw something different in this team early on. "The thing that was phenomenal about it was that nobody really had given them a chance to win that game other than themselves," he said. "When they were talking early in the week about the fact that they thought they could win the game, everybody kind of snickered. Then people realized toward the end of the week that they were serious. ESPN did a feature on College Football Game Day about Kansas State breaking the losing streak. They had the play-by-play call on that show. And I remember Coach Snyder's quote and the player quotes coming out of that feature. They were saying, 'We're going to win today.' Now everybody nationally kind of snickered as well. But that was the start of telling everybody that things were different at Kansas State. They went up to Lincoln thinking they could win."

The loss did have a detrimental effect, however. Following the game, the Cats were down to 49 scholarship players, including only two healthy defensive linemen. Of the 49, 10 were restricted from contact during practice, due to injuries. Of the 49, 21 were freshmen, either true freshmen or redshirt freshmen.

Instead, he opted for Kansas State and a similar opportunity, but with the promise of earning a scholarship. After a redshirt year in 1987 and a frustrating 1988, Smith was ready to call it quits when Stan Parrish resigned as coach. Sitting at home during the summer, he was prepared to give Tulane a shot when two things happened. First, his parents gave him their advice, and then, Coach Snyder called.

"He took a chance on me by giving me a scholarship, and I figured I'd take a chance on this guy," Smith said. "I feel that if somebody is going to look out for me, I'm going to look out for him. Then the fact that I had developed great relationships at K-State with guys like Frank Hernandez, Paul Watson, and those guys I met when I came here. It might have been a time for me when I probably would have been giving up football, and that was my first love. That's how I decided to come back."

Smith says he knew that things would improve at Kansas State. He also says he knew that it would take time. "He wasn't making any promises

that we were going to the Orange Bowl in one year," Smith recalled. "He said 'I want you to be a part of the greatest turnaround in college football.' He said, 'It's probably not going to happen within two years, but you can be a building block. Hopefully, if things do go well, you will be a part of it.'

"I went out a winner, and I was able to come back and be a part of a bowl game victory (as an undergraduate assistant). I think that reflects the confidence that Coach Snyder has in me, and the fact that he and I developed such a great relationship in the three years I played for him."

Smith gives Snyder all the credit in changing him from an overlooked high school player to a college star and now a projected starter in the Canadian Football League. The difference is attitude. "Coach Snyder stresses that we don't put any limitations on ourselves," he said. "As a 17-year-old kid, getting overlooked coming out of high school, maybe I sat at home a couple of times saying, 'Maybe I'm not as good as I think I

am.' When I got here, he said, 'Michael, you could be the greatest receiver who ever played, if you really believe in yourself. You have to work hard to get there.' He pushed me, along with Coach (Del) Miller and the rest of the staff. They pushed me so hard that I think I did reach my full potential.

That potential is still being realized. And it also gives him more than a little satisfaction on his return trips to New Orleans. "Now when I go home and I've got my bowl ring on, I say to them, 'I told you so; it takes time, but I was a part of it.' I was happy to be here for it."

Happy to have you here, Michael.

"If one more offensive lineman had been injured in the Nebraska game, we would not have had enough to finish the game," Snyder said. "We had well organized practices, because we couldn't have survived if they weren't well organized. But we couldn't have the kind of practices that would allow you to practice a shorter period of time or allow for each individual to be working exclusively on the things in which he was going to be involved.

"Youngsters today have no idea how hard those other guys had to work. We were on practice fields for long periods of time. We had a lot of meetings, long meetings. We put in a lot of effort, a lot of time, and our players put in a lot of time and a lot of effort. Surely when you do that and then you lose, it's awful easy to say, 'Why is this all necessary?'"

The numbers got so low that the offensive starters had to practice against the defensive starters, with the two units taking turns being the scout team for the other. "That means that in 50 percent of your practice, the offense is doing something it doesn't do in a game and 50 percent of the time, the defense is doing something it doesn't do," Snyder said.

That put a program already looking up at nearly every other program in the country at a further disadvantage. Taking away half their preparation time hardly seemed the remedy to put a stop to a three-year conference losing streak.

Snyder had a solution. It wouldn't help the 1989 Cats, but if his proposal were accepted, the Wildcats of 1990 and beyond would benefit greatly. Snyder proposed to the NCAA that programs competing under the 95-scholarship limit could make up the difference equally over a two-year period. That meant the Cats, and other programs like theirs, not only could sign the maximum 25 players for the following season, but split the difference between their new total and 95.

"It was apparent to me that everybody had great compassion to what our plight was, but had no intention whatsoever of trying to allow us the opportunity of getting back on our feet through the scholarship process," Snyder said when recalling the peril his team was under. It was a catch-22. Not only were the Cats shorthanded to start each game, which often led to an uneven contest, but the shortage of numbers, and Snyder's lack of qualified reserves, made the contest even more lopsided because Kansas State players got more tired, much more quickly. That fatigue led to several injuries that may have been avoided if the players were fresh.

Snyder's proposal was not adopted, but the numbers were evened slightly when the NCAA began lowering the scholarship limits in 1991. Schools were allowed 93 in 1992, 88 in 1993 and 85 for the upcoming season, when Kansas State will finally have a full contingent. It wasn't the solution Snyder was looking for, but it made the field a little more level.

Seniors like Erick Harper felt a renewed enthusiasm under Coach Bill Snyder.

If there are schools that still are struggling to reach the quota, Snyder is totally in favor of helping them out. "I don't want anybody to have to go through what we went through," he said.

The week after the loss to Nebraska, the Cats ventured to Oklahoma State for a tussle with the Cowboys. The Cowboys had struggled to a 1-4 start and starting quarterback Mike Gundy was on the sideline with a bruised knee. The Wildcats took advantage. They claimed a 13-3 halftime lead behind two David Kruger field goals and a 1-yard run by Antoine Dulan.

But late in the third quarter with OSU behind 13-10, Gundy decided his knee wasn't bad enough to keep him from contributing. He limped onto the field and engineered three drives, the final one being the game-winner. His first drive led the Cowboys to the KSU 3 where they were stopped on downs. On the next series, he completed a 21-yard pass,

end, the position at which he was recruited out of Wichita North High School. And he hit the practice fields, over and over again. "I caught a ton of balls," he said.

"A lot of my motivation came from the fact that I am a Christian. I wanted to honor God with football. I wanted to do well, because I knew that everybody knew that I was a Christian. I cared what people thought about the Lord. I didn't want to look like a pansy. I really wanted to honor God with what I did. It wasn't all that pure. I also was an athlete and I didn't want to look like a pansy."

Football was secondary for Campbell. His faith was most important.

Russ Campbell always had plenty of talent. It just was well hidden deep inside his 6-5, 255-pound frame.

Campbell was a struggling sophomore defensive end for first-year coach Bill Snyder, when he questioned his ultimate "head coach" about whether he even should be playing at all. "I was pretty close to just saying, well, 'I quit,'" he said. "I was chewing on that decision for a long time. I kept asking God what I should do. I decided that if I did keep playing, I had to give it my best."

So Campbell decided to stick around. He was switched back to tight

but the receiver coughed up the ball.

Finally, with about five minutes remaining, Gundy began a drive on his own 9. He marched the Cowboys down to the KSU 15 from where he hit Brent Parker for the score with 1:37 left.

"He was a tremendous quarterback, and it was one of those things where we had just not learned how to win yet," Snyder said. Then he added, without trying to make excuses, "We were down to two defensive lineman (the formation called for three), and had to play someone out of position."

Victory was sweet for the win-starved Cats of 1989.

With visions of North Texas dancing in their heads, the Cats took over on their own 20. Straw led the Cats to the OSU 45 with 12 seconds left. He threw a pass to Hernandez in the end zone, but it fell incomplete with five seconds remaining. On the

Shortly after arriving at K-State, he became involved in the Fellowship of Christian Athletes. He was a team leader who used his role on the team to further his ministry. "I think I had a lot of freedom because I was ministering to my peers," he said. "I always tried to promote it among my teammates. It was a tool for evangelism.

"I was involved in the FCA in high school, but I became real involved at K-State because of Coach (Jerry) Palmieri. We became really good friends. Being a Christian was an important thing for both Coach Palmieri and me."

Campbell said he and Snyder "sometimes talked about what it meant to be a Christian and the way the Lord was working in our lives."

Campbell's faith played a role in his decision to stay at K-State. "He was a guy for a while who was a fish out of water," Snyder said. "He wasn't sure whether he needed to stay, wanted to stay or should stay. Russ is a guy who struggles with a lot of decisions. Most of his decisions are made through his faith, and through prayer. The Lord kept him here, kept him working.

"He has a tremendous work ethic. He's always going to do the things you ask of him, plus he's going to do a little bit more. That sets him apart from the average player. He made himself into a very, very fine football player. And he always kept things in perspective. As much as he wanted to go on and play at the professional level, he

always kept his life in perspective. He's always been a very sound young guy.

"He also always tried very hard to help other people. That's a part of his life. He feels that there is that need for him to do that and he does. He's done a lot of things. He's volunteered his time with the church to help young people. He worked with a lot of the players in our program.

"He's a missionary in a helmet, a very special young man."

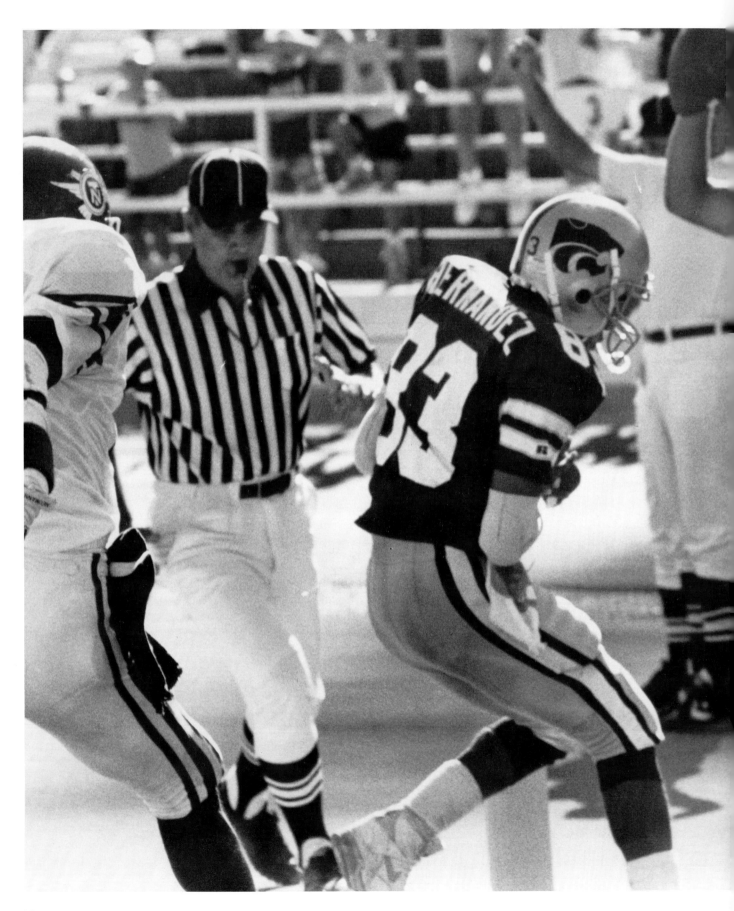

final play, Straw sent everybody into the end zone. But while scrambling away from the rush, he stepped over the line of scrimmage and had to run. He made it to the 29, where the game ended.

The effort was one to be admired. The Cats were so thin that several freshmen who were supposed to redshirt were suited up ready to play. In fact, Jaime Mendez, a safety who was redshirting, was preparing to go into the game. Had he gotten into the action, it would have sacrificed his redshirt season, but secondary coach Bobby Stoops changed his mind and held Mendez out of the game.

"I have great respect for the players who stayed on the field when it would have been easy for them to jump in the tank and let one of these other guys come in and suffer the brunt of it," Snyder said. "There were guys who were playing 80 snaps a ballgame, because they were trying to help save somebody's redshirt year or because there simply was no one left to take their place.

"Our goal for the 1989 season was to get as many games as possible into the fourth quarter with a chance to win. We did that six times, but won only one. We knew that we were making headway, but just didn't have the numbers to sustain our efforts for a full 60 minutes.

"I was proud, not only of the players who stayed with the program and worked hard to improve, but also of our coaches and support staff because of their perseverance. They never gave up and, like the players, were highly motivated to move into the 1990 season with greater expectations."

Kansas State closed out the 1989 season with one win. But they no longer were the Mildcats. They believed in themselves and their ability to win. The greatest turnaround in college football history had begun.

Several sets of eyes made sure Frank Hernandez got a foot inbounds on "The Catch."

1990

THE 15-YARD OUT

Five wins is a modest goal. For Kansas State, it was a goal that had not been achieved since 1982, and only one time had the Wildcats achieved it since 1973.

But heading into the 1990 season, Kansas State didn't blink at the possibility of winning five games. "We knew we were going to get better," head coach Bill Snyder said.

So when the Cats squared off against the Missouri Tigers in Week 7, the fact that there were *bowl scouts* in the crowd didn't faze the 4-2 Wildcats.

"It was an indication that some progress had been made, and I wanted our players to have respect for that," Snyder said. "But it certainly didn't warrant any more than a fleeting second of thought and then it was a matter of getting on to business."

The Wildcats lost the game, 31-10, and the bowl talk subsided for another year. But the fact that bowl games were looking into the Wildcats a little more than one year after they snapped a 30-game winless streak spoke volumes about the progress that had

The Cats' swarming defense nearly made Western Illinois their first shutout victim in 17 years.

been made.

The 1990 season started with two wins, and three wins in the first four games, for the first time since 1982. Originally, the Cats were supposed to have games against the likes of Florida, Tennessee, Ohio State, Clemson and Washington in Snyder's first few years. Former athletic director Larry Travis had scheduled those games with the idea of a big pay day for the Cats. But Snyder saw no reason to sacrifice his players for the sake of the cash drawer. So he dropped many of the games and exchanged them with games against teams "on a level playing field."

While Snyder came under some criticism for a weaker schedule, he never felt the need to apologize. "If you're trying to experience losing, they'd already experienced that," he said. "That wasn't going to help. What they needed to experience was some degree of success. The only opportunity they were going to have to have any degree of success was to be able to play what at least were comparable opponents."

The first such contest pitted the Western Illinois Leathernecks against the Cats. Much had been made about the progress Kansas State had made in Snyder's first year, and even though it resulted in only one win, much more was expected in 1990. Western Illinois would be a good test to see if expectation could meet reality.

The Cats passed. Both the ball and the first test. Carl Straw passed for 246 yards and Paul Watson added 63 yards. Frank Hernandez and Michael Smith became the first pair of Wildcats each to gain more than 100 receiving yards in the same game, with 137 and 107 yards, respectively. The defense held the Leathernecks to 127 yards of total offense and forced six turnovers in nearly recording their first shutout in 15 years. There were mistakes made – three Straw interceptions in Western Illinois territory and the fact that the defense allowed nine of 20 third-down conversions – but the Cats were 1-0, matching the win total for 1989 and exceeding that of the two previous years.

"Western Illinois had a decent team," Mitch Holthus, the "Voice of the Wildcats" said. "They had a guy – Brian Cox – who's now in the NFL with the Miami Dolphins. But I could see that Coach Snyder's formula was being put into motion. They were play-ing a pretty good I-AA team and didn't play well, but they still won. That had not hap-

While the offense was effective against Western Illinois, it exploded against New Mexico State which enthused the defense as well.

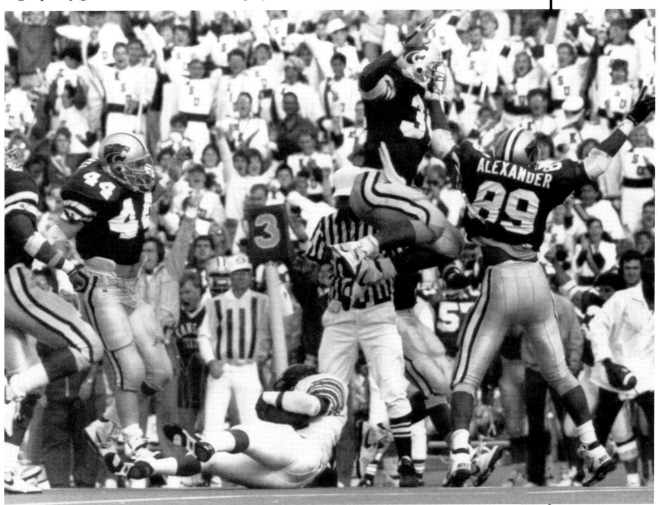

pened in a long, long time."

Two wins into Snyder's coaching career and there still were many losing streaks remaining. The next to go was a four-year streak to Division I-A teams. The last I-A win was against Kansas in 1986, the last win of any kind before the 30-game streak. New Mexico State presented a good opportunity to end that skid, considering the Aggies owned the nation's longest current losing streak at 19 games.

End it the Wildcats did. They streaked to a 42-0 halftime lead and smoked the

Aggies, 52-7. The numbers were staggering. The Cats rolled to 489 yards of total offense, including 303 yards on the ground. Pat Jackson rushed for 156 of those yards and tied a school record with four rushing touchdowns.

It hardly seemed possible that a year before, Snyder was answering questions about how the Wildcats had extended their winless skein to 29 games with a loss to Division I-AA Northern Iowa in the season's second week. In 1990, after two weeks the Wildcats were 2-0 and Snyder was answering questions on why he piled on the score.

"There's not a (coach) in the country who is going to take his number ones out in the first half," he said when quizzed following the game.

It wasn't just the starters who pummeled the Aggies. Second- and third-string players continued to pour it on. The Wildcats ran most of the second half and still outscored New Mexico State, 10-7. The Aggies lone score came after Kansas State's only turnover.

"I think those comments were tongue-in-cheek," Snyder said of the questions about running up the score. "Of all the games that we have played, that might have been as much of a surprising ballgame to us as any we have played. I thought they were going to be a pretty formidable opponent. I think we caught them off balance a little bit and our players played very well and gained momentum very quickly."

The Cats traveled to Dekalb, Illinois, for a rematch with Northern Illinois in the third week, and let a 14-point, fourth-quarter lead slip away. Stacey Robinson scored

Mention the name Carl Straw to anyone connected with the Kansas State football program from 1987 to 1990 and they'll talk about toughness. Mention toughness to Carl Straw and he'll just shrug it off.

"The pain tolerance that I had when playing the game was, well, I didn't feel it," he says. "I was on such a high to play the game that it didn't matter. Sunday was the day to hurt. So if I broke a finger or twisted an ankle in the first quarter, it's not going to take me out of the game. Just tape it up, let's go. Sunday morning you can barely walk. You'd have to crawl to the bathroom, but I felt a responsibility to the team to be there and to play every snap no matter how hard I got hit, no matter how many nosebleeds I got. This is the way I am."

Keep in mind when Straw says that it didn't matter if he twisted an ankle or broke a finger that he was the starting quarterback. A player who has to be able to use all five fingers to grip the ball to throw it properly. A player who has to be able to run, in Straw's case, away from the constant defensive pressure. "I didn't run that much," he joked. "I was able to backpedal."

Straw learned his toughness at an early age. He had two sisters and no brothers, but he took up football at age 5. "My first coach was Mike Campanella," he said. "He was such a hard guy that he basically scared it into me never to miss a snap. Then every coach after him put it into me, 'You're the captain, you're the guy everybody looks up to, so you can't get hurt.'

"So when I finally got to college, if I got hurt, I got hurt. But there was no way you were going to take me out of the game. I had been playing football since I was 5, so the tolerance to pain was pretty great. I would have to break something like a major bone or something to come out, because you sprain fingers, little things."

Straw had plenty of practice shrugging off "little things" at Kansas State. He was the winner of the team's Ken Ochs Courage Award in 1989, no doubt for taking a pounding so often and getting back up for more. "He was really a very hard-nosed guy," Coach Bill Snyder said. "There may be some who have a great degree of toughness. The thing that set Carl apart was the fact that Carl never complained

about anything. His ankles were taped like a Clydesdale. He was banged up frequently, and that was a period of time when he was taking more of a beating than most quarterbacks would. Yet he was always right back on his feet again, and he never said a word about it. His toughness allowed him to be a very strong leader in our program."

Straw developed with the Kansas State program. He redshirted in 1986, the last time that Kansas State won a game before Snyder got to Manhattan. He played in four games as a freshman and started nine games as a sophomore. An injury limited him to five games in 1989 – no, it was not a decapitation, but it was a badly sprained ankle. One of the games he did play was the thrilling last-second victory over North Texas, when he led an 85-yard drive in the final 1:31 capped by his pass to Frank Hernandez on the final play.

Even his toughness did not prepare him for the aftermath. "I didn't see him catch it," Straw said. "I got tackled. All I heard was this roar. I was still on the ground and all of a sudden I got tackled by about 20 people. They

the game-winning touchdown with 40 seconds remaining as the Huskies edged Kansas State, 42-35.

K-State did well offensively, rushing for 127 yards and passing for 327. Carl Straw helped the Cats jump to a 28-13 half-time lead by completing 14 of 16 passes for 163 yards before intermission. But Robinson, who led the Huskies with 152 yards rushing, owned the fourth quarter.

"It was a disheartening loss, because coming off New Mexico State, we really felt, and our players felt, that they were arriving," Snyder said. "Again, the lesson that we learned from

were all fans. For 10 minutes, I couldn't get off the ground. I couldn't breathe because everybody was jumping on me."

In 1990, Straw got to be a part of five wins, the most in his career. The key to the offense Snyder instituted when he arrived is an effective quarterback. The quarterback has to read the defense and then throw to an area. It is then the responsibility of the receiver to get to the ball.

Straw gives credit to Snyder for giving him an offense that would allow him to flourish. "It's not a difficult system to learn," he said. "You're taught the audibles first. The name of the play comes later. They signal it in. You pick it up as an audible and you call it in the huddle as a play. If it's taught that way, it's a lot easier to grasp when you're up on the line and you have to call a different play.

"Coach Snyder gives football back to the players. He makes the gameplan, but the game is controlled by the players. A coach can only call a play. Now if you give the responsibility to the players to change that play, in split seconds they can change a play to a better one because they can see a lot more on the field."

Straw says his main strength was making the proper read and throwing the ball to the right area. "There are five or six reads that you have to make," he said. "If you get through all of them, you'll be okay.

"It's just a matter of being tough. You're going to get hit when you throw the ball."

And if you're Carl Straw, you simply get back up.

that was that once things begin to get on a roll, when you're feeling pretty good about yourself, you better be careful because there's somebody lurking around the corner. It's one of those 'don't take anything for granted' messages."

The defense shone for the third time in four games against New Mexico, as the Wildcats completed a 3-1 non-conference schedule with a 38-6 pasting. The Cats' D forced six turnovers and recorded six sacks, two more than it had in the first three games combined. Also, for the third time in four games, the Wildcats held their opponent to single digits, the first time that had occurred since the bowl year of 1982. In fact, the Wildcats had not held a single opponent under 10 points since the 1986 opener.

"Our defense really rose to the occasion in the second half," Snyder said. "For us to have a chance to win, our defense has to force turnovers and eliminate the big plays."

The offense also performed capably, gaining 396 yards without committing a turnover. Watson came in for Straw, who suffered an ankle sprain, and led the Cats to three second-half scoring drives. He scored two of the TDs himself on runs of 40 and 2 yards. He finished the game with 66 yards on the ground and 114 yards passing, completing six of his 11 attempts.

Michael Smith also continued to rise on the KSU receiving charts, as he caught seven passes for 179 yards. He finished nine yards shy of Dave Jones' school record.

"This is a great win, but it doesn't mean we have turned the corner," Snyder said after the Wildcats matched their bowl-year pre-conference mark of 3-1. "We still have a maze in front of us, but this win tells us that we're going in the right direction."

The improvement can be traced directly to the Wildcats ability to grasp Snyder's complex offensive scheme. The 15-yard Out is the trademark play in the offense. "If you look at the history of Coach at

Defense was the key for the Cats in 1990 as they built their best start since 1982.

A new weight room (following pages) gave Kansas State one of the best-equipped facilities in the conference.

Iowa and here, you'll see that his prototype quarterbacks are tough kids physically, first of all," Holthus said. "Carl was that way. Chad (May) is that way. Watson was at the end of his career. Chuck Long was. Mark Vlassic was. Chuck Hartleib was. They also have to be strong enough mentally and understand the game well enough to make great decisions under considerable pressure.

"A quarterback has a lot of freedom in Coach's system, but it's very complicated. It's Calculus III. They have to understand the game of football enough to be able to run the right play at the right spot. The quarterback has to be strong enough to throw the 15-yard out. That seems like a simple play to the football fan, but it's really not. He has to have a strong arm and he has to be able to throw to a spot near the boundary. The receiver has to be able to execute the play. There's so much air between the quarterback and the receiver. You can't leave a lot of air under the ball.

"It's a tough play to defend, too. If you can throw that pass, it's impossible to defend. You can run that play all day long, if you're executing

Joe Boone always had something to prove. Not recruited by a major college out of high school, he went to Coffeyville Junior College. At Coffeyville, he was told that he had no chance to play big-time college football. And standing just 6-1, he was told he was too small when he finally did sign on with a Division I-A school.

But Boone only was interested in proving himself to one person. The man in the mirror.

"I wasn't really out to prove anything to anyone except myself," he said. "I had felt that it was a level at which I could play."

Boone had experienced a rough year at Coffeyville. At home at linebacker, he was tried at all seven defensive front positions. "My coach said that it's a pretty slim chance I'd make it anywhere in the Big Eight or any other big school," he said. "He said I should stick with some of the smaller schools. I wasn't happy there. I felt I should have been playing more."

Boone left Coffeyville after one season and walked on to Kansas State in the spring of 1989. Not coincidentally, it was the same spring that Bill Snyder conducted his first practice in Manhattan. "Both KU and K-State were getting new coaching staffs," he said. "The coaching staffs during my four years in high school were trying to pull the athletes from Florida and Texas and not even worry about Kansas. I knew that when Coach Snyder got in here he would start concentrating on Kansas. If you wanted to keep the fans at home, you had to keep the players at home. You started to see a lot of players from

it properly. And then if you do run that play, it sets up a plethora of other things to do. In Carl, Coach had a guy who was strong enough to throw that play, strong enough physically and mentally to do the things that he wanted in his offense."

The next addition to the football facilities also occurred in 1990. A new weight room was constructed prior to the season. For years, the Wildcats went up against conference opponents who were bigger and stronger. While the Cats would scratch and claw for three quarters, endurance was a problem and they would wither down the stretch. Strength and conditioning often made the difference between winning and losing.

"In the past in the fourth quarter, Kansas State would hang with the opponent as long as it could, but then the players would run out of gas," KSU strength and conditioning coach Rod Cole said of the weight room now. "We are developing the power to play football. We do a lot of the Olympic lifts – cleans, snatches,

Kansas stepping up and playing just because Coach Snyder kept some of the scholarships at home for them."

The transition was a tough one for Boone. He never had been a part of a losing program. Coffeyville was rated in the Top 10 throughout his year there. At Aquinas High School in Lenexa, Kansas, he was a part of a state runner-up team. But his first year at Kansas State, the Wildcats were 1-10. Yet, he never had second thoughts about his decision.

"No, not one bit," he said. "That 1-10 year hurt, and it showed. But you could see where Coach Snyder was going with this program. It was a weeding out process. He had to weed out some of the people who weren't going to do what it takes to win." That was hard work.

"You really can't go through Coach Snyder's program without working your butt off," Boone continued. "It just can't be done. Even in the off-season. I think the off-season is tougher than playing the games during the 11-game season. The running and the lifting, there is no easy part."

Boone also realized that nothing was expected of the players that wasn't demanded of the coaching staff. "You've got to hand it to the coaching

staff," he said. "They work 80 hours a week, and they get it done. They put us in a position to win. It's up to the players to do it or not. Granted we go through all the running and hitting, but they're the brains behind it, and they're the ones who put us in that position to get it done."

Boone was put in a position where he became the second-leading tackler on the team his senior season with 89 stops. "Joe Boone was an extremely competitive young man who, like many of the linebackers here, would never give up," Snyder said of the one-time walk-on. "He always believed we would win, and because of his toughness and work ethic he provided great leadership for his teammates."

Boone gives specific credit to former defensive coordinator Bob Cope. Each week, Cope would single out one defensive play that cost the Cats points, and subsequently control of the game. "He was one guy who really set the foundation as far as the defense goes," Boone said. "He showed us that one blown play, mentally, and the other team makes a big play. It makes them look so much better and it makes us look bad. He wanted to make us realize that we were in control, and we

could control the outcome of the game."

It all comes back to discipline. When players would skip a class or a study hall, or be late for a team meeting, they would have to run the stadium stairs eight times, run eight 100-yard dashes and then eight 100-yard "up and downs," where the player dropped at five-yard intervals. Boone believes that the discipline for off-field transgressions built unity on the field.

"Once you get in there, you can look at your teammates when the huddle breaks and you know that they're going to get their job done," he said. "You have that sense of teamwork, and that's something that they really build into you. You really have to trust the guy next to you to get his job done."

By the time Joe Boone's career was done at Kansas State, he had proved to everyone he could be trusted to do his.

clean and jerks – that are quick lifts in the weight room that develop attributes that carry over to the football field. There are a lot of ways to train a football team. We try to draw the best from each way."

Heading into the 1990 Big Eight season, there still were question marks. The strength of the non-conference schedule placed an asterisk by the 3-1 mark, even though the victories were decisive. The Wildcats had not beaten a conference team since 1986, and the people were wondering just how far a positive attitude could take them.

Against Nebraska, only about a half. The Wildcats still were feeling the effects of a shortage in numbers. They held NU to just 64 yards of total offense until the 2:19 mark of the first half, but then gave up an 11-play, 81-yard drive that was capped by a touchdown in the final seconds to give the Huskers a 10-2 halftime lead.

The second half belonged to Nebraska, as the Huskers outscored K-State, 35-6, in that stanza. The real hero units for Nebraska, however, were the special teams. The punt- and kickoff-return teams amassed 323 yards, 49 fewer than the offense. Tyrone Hughes ran one kickoff 99 yards for a score as part of a 21-point fourth quarter.

The Cats lined up against Oklahoma State the following week with a chance for a first. No current KSU player ever had been an active part of a conference victory. Straw and back-up quarterback Chris Cobb both were redshirting freshmen in 1986 when the Cats defeated Kansas, 29-12. And if not for the heroics of Chris Patterson, none would yet have been involved in a Big Eight win.

The Wildcats held a tenuous 23-17 lead over the Cowboys midway through the fourth quarter. Oklahoma State took nine plays to drive to the KSU 10-yard line, from where it faced a third-and-goal. OSU back-up QB Kenny Ford was flushed from the pocket, but found his way toward the goal line. He appeared to be heading in for the tying score, but Patterson stripped the ball just before he crossed the line. Danny Needham recovered the loose ball at the Cats 15-yard line and the Cowboys' last threat was stopped.

"I wasn't in position to make a hit, but I had a chance to go for the ball, for a strip," Patterson

Chris Patterson (34) and Jody Kilian handled the Oklahoma State offense and the KSU offense scored enough points to earn a Big Eight victory.

77

said. "It worked. It was a diving, desperation type of play. I just grabbed his arm and slid down to rake the ball."

Although it was the biggest play of the day, it was not the only reason the Cats prevailed for the first time in 28 conference games. The Wildcats' secondary held OSU's quarterbacks to nine of 29 passing for 78 yards and two interceptions. The defense rose up big on two other occasions when Okie State had a chance to grab the momentum.

Late in the first half, Pat Jackson fumbled at his own 28-yard line with less than two minutes remaining and the Cowboys benefiting from a 20- to 25-mph wind at their backs. The Cowboys had three straight incompletions and failed to get off a 45-yard field goal attempt because of a bad snap.

In the third quarter, again with the wind at their backs, the Cowboys scored quickly, taking a 17-10 lead on a Cecil Wilson 1-yard run. After a short punt, OSU had the ball at the K-State 34. But two more incompletions and a Patterson tackle of Gerald Hudson seven yards behind the line of scrimmage forced the Cowboys to punt.

The Wildcats then marched 80 yards against the wind in 14 plays to tie the score on Rod Schiller's 1-yard run. Straw then gave KSU its final points on a 1-yard run with 11:24 remaining.

But all that seemed for naught as Ford drove the Cowboys against the wind deep into Kansas State territory. Visions of the previous year's comeback by OSU, the loss to Northern Illinois earlier in the year and countless other heartbreaking finishes lurked in the minds of KSU faithful.

"Everyone was talking about who was going to make a big play," Needham said. "In the past, we've just waited for someone else to make the play. All the credit goes to Chris. The guy had a touchdown."

"It was a very important play in the history of this particular program," Snyder said. "I think the perception was that Kansas State always could find a way to lose, and here we found a way to win." The perception was changing.

The win lifted the Cats to 4-2 and assured them of their first winning season at home since 1984. It also moved them into bowl consideration as they prepared for Missouri.

"I'm flattered," said then-Kansas State director of athletics Steve Miller. "I didn't think we'd be talking about bowl games this early. I'm thrilled about the bowl. I would like to feel Bill is a little more excited than he's putting on. This is what you get into the business for. That's what you play the game for."

Snyder had approached the bowl talk with his usual reserve. He was honored by the attention, but wasn't so sure the Cats were ready for it. "I'm not sure why they'll be there, probably to see the (2-4) University of Missouri," he quipped. "If they come to see us, we're honored, obviously. But it's a little early for that."

The Tigers proved that to be true. They jumped out to a 17-3 halftime lead en route to a 31-10 victory. The Wildcats managed to get inside the Missouri 40-yard line five times but only could get the 10 points. "I don't think that we had done anything to prove that we were necessarily a bowl team," Snyder recalled. That certainly proved to be true. "I think we were capable of competing better against Missouri than we did at that time. We played very poorly there both defensively and offensively."

The Cats also came up short against arch-rival Kansas the following week. Kansas built a 27-10 third-quarter lead, capped by a 58-yard Dan Eichloff field goal, before withstanding a fierce KSU rally. After the Wildcats scored their final points, making

Despite being only 5′ 9″, Pat Jackson was a threat out of the backfield for the Cats.

the score 27-24, Kansas held onto the ball for the final minutes.

The two straight losses to Big Eight teams left the Wildcats feeling a little low heading into the final home contest against Iowa State. The fact that the temperature was in the low 40s with a stiff wind carrying a cold rain certainly could have made even the most optimistic fan shudder. But Snyder actually was pleased with the weather conditions.

"What I told our players, and what I've always told them, is that we are an inclement weather football team," Snyder said. "That's like playing at home; that's your place. Inclement weather is our trademark and we always want it to be. That's where we have to start. If we got days like that one, that's a bonus."

Focus is one of those overused words in sports. Players talk about getting focused on their goals. Teams talk about keeping their focus, too. But there isn't a more appropriate word to describe Kansas State's standout defensive end Reggie Blackwell. Blackwell is focused.

That really is saying a lot, too. You see, Blackwell was born without a right eye. "I never really looked at it as

an obstacle," he said. "I've played football since I was 8 years old. I looked at it as a motivational tool. I'm the youngest of nine kids. I have six older brothers, all of whom played football before me, and they all treated me the same.

"The main thing is that I couldn't dwell on something that I couldn't control. I accepted that this was going to be a part of my life the rest of my life

and was something that I needed to deal with. I could have gone in two directions. I could have looked at it as a handicap and wanted to have people feel sorry for me. Or I could go in another direction and just say, 'This is a part of my life. This is really not a handicap. You're just as normal as anybody else,' and just go on and continue with life. That's the way I looked at it."

Blackwell certainly learned to deal with it very well. In his senior year of high school in St. Louis, he recorded 101 solo tackles, including 11 quarterback sacks, earning him numerous post-season honors, including all-state. He was the senior class president and was a member of the national honor society. It was his ability to look past the obstacle and focus on the future that convinced Snyder that Blackwell could play college ball.

"Sometimes, these problems might have made it rather difficult to pursue and recruit a youngster," Snyder said. "But it wasn't a handicap

The game was close, only for a half. Iowa State led, 14-7, at halftime and chose to take the wind in the third quarter. That backfired as the first of three key plays gave the Wildcats the decisive points. Rogerick Green intercepted a tipped ball at the Cyclones 30-yard line on the second play from scrimmage. Six plays later, Jackson rumbled in from the 1.

After an exchange of punts, Chris Cobb pinned Iowa State on their own 4. On the second play, Sundiata Patterson fumbled and Chris Patterson recovered on the 1. Richard Boyd ran it in on second down. Finally, Iowa State, faced with fourth-and-seven from the Wildcats 47 faked a punt. William Price read the fake and tackled the punter for a 6-yard loss. On the first play, Straw hit tight end Al Jones with a 47-yard strike and the game was out of reach.

Snyder's approach instilled confidence in the team. "I told them the football team that had the toughest quarterback on that given day was going to win this football game," Snyder said. "And I said, 'There shouldn't be a doubt in anybody's mind as to who has the toughest quarterback.'

"The quarterback who was best geared to handle the elements certainly was not going to be as prone to turning the ball over and doing things that would get you beat. And in that type of weather, first you have to make sure you don't do those things to beat yourself, and I felt that Carl would be tough enough not to do that. And I honestly believed that our players gravitated to Carl's toughness."

"He had me up in his office before we even went down to the lockerroom," Straw said. "I started taping and he says, 'We're going to win this game.' I said, 'What?!' He

for Reggie, and consequently we felt comfortable recruiting him."

Most people who know Snyder know that he only recruits people he believes can handle the task of being a *student*-athlete. Snyder had no doubt that Blackwell could handle that, too. "He always was a positive guy," Snyder said. "He was able, mentally, really to focus on what it would take for him to overcome that impediment. He was a diverse young man. He did a lot of different things. He was president of his fraternity and provided leadership in that capacity. He was a good student and he was a pleasant young fellow with a good personality who provided some leadership on our football team."

Blackwell took his school work seriously. He believed that the free education his football ability provided for him was his ticket out of the tough times he endured as a youth. He gives Snyder credit for stressing the need for self-discipline off the field as well as on.

"Coach Snyder always checked with you on a daily basis," he said. "He wanted to know how we were doing academically. Coach talked a lot about discipline. He had rules like no earrings, no hats in the building, being five minutes early to meetings and things of that nature. It helped me to realize that football is great, but not everybody is going to the NFL. Only two percent of all college players go to the NFL. I just had to look at that and wake up myself and say, 'I'd better go in and take care of business academically, because this will be over in no time.'

"When Coach Snyder gave me a scholarship, he gave me an opportunity. A lot of people don't look at that as getting four or five years of free education. I grew up in the inner-city of St. Louis and I knew I had to try to take advantage of it. There was no reason for me to go to college for four or five years and then come back to the same situation."

Blackwell was chastised by a lot

of friends and family for choosing Kansas State. When he signed, he was being pursued by Missouri and Illinois, and Kansas State was completing its second straight winless season. But Blackwell saw something at K-State.

"Visiting K-State and going through the recruiting trip with Coach Snyder, he emphasized that it was a good academic school and there also was the opportunity to play quickly," he said. "I could see the support he was getting from the outside, as far as the alumni. There were the new facilities that were in the plans – the weight room, the indoor facility, the new press box and the Big Eight room – all those things in the future. So he was making an effort to provide the direction to put us in the best position where we could be successful."

It's interesting. Blackwell only had one eye. But he was able to see things that an awful lot of people with two good eyes never could see.

Frank Hernandez didn't possess blazing speed, but he had enough skill to be part of the most productive receiver combination in school history.

said, 'You love this stuff. You grew up in this stuff. I know we're going to win. You're the toughest quarterback in the league. You love this stuff.

"I was like, 'It's snowing. It's raining.' He said, 'Yes, but you can throw in it.' I was like, 'OK.'"

Actually, the Wildcats could have quit early on. After selecting the wind on the opening flip, KSU tried to give the game to Iowa State. Straw's second pass was picked off, though the Cyclones could not advance. They had to punt, but Michael Smith fumbled the punt and ISU had the ball on the KSU 21. Four plays later, all-America candidate Blaise Bryant was heading into the end zone for the go-ahead score when he left the ball behind him. He had been hit by Chris Patterson, and Jaime Mendez recovered for Kansas State. There's a familiar ring to that play.

Iowa State took a 7-0 lead in the second quarter when Bryant crossed the goal line with the ball. KSU tied the score with 2:15 remaining in the half on a Straw-to-Hernandez 19-yard pass. But ISU marched 58 yards in 1:17 to take the lead at half. Then the strong wind, and the stronger Wildcats, took over.

When Danny Needham recovered Kenny Ford's fumble, the Wildcats' first conference win since 1986 was secured.

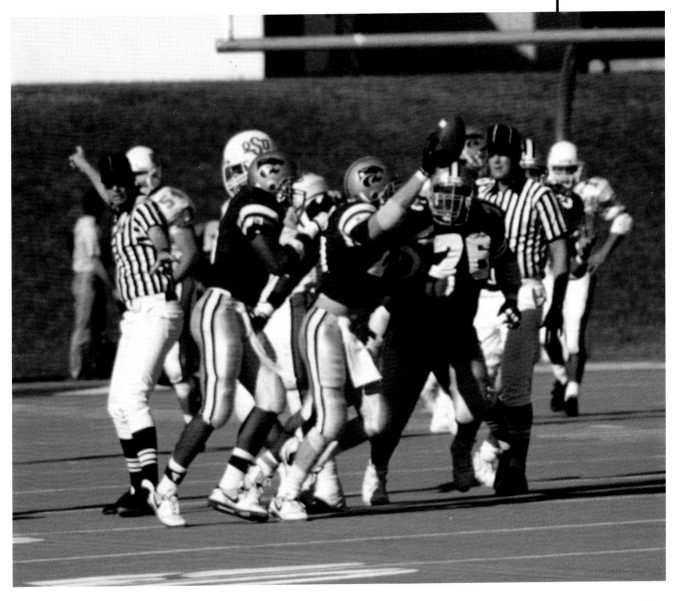

"I can remember the direction the wind was blowing the rain," Snyder said. "It was parallel to the ground. The surface was probably not as wet as you might have thought, because the rain didn't have a chance to touch the ground."

The Wildcats lost their last two games on the road, 34-7 to Oklahoma and 64-3 to eventual national champion Colorado, to finish the season at 5-6.

"It was a real embarrassment to get beaten as badly as we did at Colorado," Snyder said. "It was especially bad being the last ballgame of the year, because that's the one that you live with for a year's period of time until you get a chance to go out and redeem yourself. Normally they say there is less pain in getting beat substantially than in losing a close ballgame, but I'm here to tell you that that's not always the case. That was a very painful ballgame."

Although losing four of their last five was a disappointment to the Cats, the season showed how far the program had come. It wasn't that long before that fans tore down goal posts following a last-second win over a Division I-AA team.

The turnaround, well beyond the expectations of many so-called experts, earned Snyder the Big Eight Coach of the Year honors. "I'm just grateful that coaches and the media felt that strongly about what had taken place here," Snyder said. "It's a reflection, not any moreso on me than it is on our assistant coaches and the players. It's recognition for the entire program that something positive was taking place."

The players he is referring to also garnered some postseason honors. Michael Smith earned third-team all-America honors from *Football News*. He was one of 11 players to merit mention on one of the all-Big Eight teams, including six second-teamers. Equally important to Snyder is the fact that six players were on the Academic All-Big Eight Honor Roll.

The support of Snyder was unanimous from the players, like Rogerick Green, whose speed earned him a job in the pros and helped the Cats to a 5-6 record in 1990.

1991
CROSSING THE LINE

At the beginning of fall practice in 1991, Coach Bill Snyder invited Mitch Holthus, the "Voice of the Wildcats," to address the Kansas State football team. Holthus congratulated them on the improvement they had shown during the previous two seasons and complimented them on the promise they showed for the 1991 season. Then he said something that stuck in the mind of every player on the team: "Cross the Line."

The 1989 win, the first in 30 games, was exciting and showed that there was a fighting spirit in the program. The five wins in 1990 showed that sheer determination and guts could overcome a lack of numbers and maybe even a shortage of talent. But 1991 was the time to cross the line to better things. Namely, Holthus said, the time had come to win more games than they lost, win on the road, and most of all, defeat the University of Kansas.

"I thought it was the next logical step for the program," Holthus said, "Now I could see the metamorphosis from being a perennial 3-8 to 0-11 team to having the capability physically, being familiar enough with his system and having the players in place, that they had a chance for a winning season. I wouldn't have given the "Cross the Line" speech to the 1989 team or the 1990 team, because I don't think it would have been realistic. That's not a slap to that team. But in '89 they won a game, and in '90 they won five games and they won a league game. But they had yet to win on the road in the league, they had yet to beat Kansas and they had yet to have a winning season. That to me was the next logical step and a proper step for the program to take."

The slogan became the rallying cry for the Wildcats. "Mitch can get guys excited sometimes, especially if they haven't heard him before," Coach Bill Snyder said. "He told them they needed to cross the line, and then defined what he meant by that, and it caught their attention. I didn't want to lose a moment, so I had it painted on the locker-room wall where they walk out to go onto the field.

Thanks to a winning lottery ticket for Dave and Carol Wagner, KSU Stadium had a new turf and a new name in 1991.

That was kind of a phrase that repeated itself frequently during the season. It was a beneficial piece of motivation throughout the season."

For Quentin Neujahr, as for many of the players, it merely put into words what they already were thinking. "I think we had crossed the line before the season even started," Neujahr said. "Just the attitude of players in the off-season was better. We worked harder than any of the two years before, without a doubt. We were ready to take the next step, from better than average team to good team."

While the Cats had great plans for 1991, the Big Eight Skywriters, a group of reporters and broadcasters who travel to each preseason camp in the conference and then report on their findings, figured the Cats had to prove it. They tabbed the Purples for eighth place, a kind of tradition around the Big Eight. "That's how the vote has come out in the last 123 years in succession," Snyder said. "I just don't think anyone wanted to be the one to alter that. My only response is that it's something that is done every year and very seldom does it turn out correct. I just hope that this one doesn't either."

It didn't.

(From the left): Michael Smith, Russ Campbell and Frank Hernandez became the Big Eight's first trio of 1,000-yard receivers on the same team.

The Cats did cross the line in 1991, and not just by sticking a big toe over it. They leaped over it. By the time the season was done, Snyder had earned his second straight Big Eight Coach of the Year honor and was named ESPN's National Coach of the Year by leading Kansas State to its best record since 1954. Yet Snyder was not satisfied. A break here and there and the Wildcats would have spent New Year's Day, 1992, in Miami at the Orange Bowl.

"We told the players we were less than two feet short of the Orange Bowl," Snyder said, with his tongue only slightly embedded in his cheek. "I'm really not big on would have, could have scenarios. I've always tried to bring up to our football teams a number of things that allow them to learn, to realize what can take place, how good they can be.

"In the Nebraska ballgame we missed a controversial field goal by that much," he said with his fingers three inches apart. "We put that in perspective and said if we had that particular field goal, that put us up by 10 points against Nebraska and changes the field position and puts us in a very, very positive position. (Right before the field goal attempt) Eric Gallon takes the handoff on third-and-two on the Nebraska 16, and the (hole in the line) opens up. He slips on the turf and he's down and we have to try a kick. If he plants his foot a few inches over, maybe he doesn't slip and we score a touchdown.

"Then, when we played Colorado, Colorado crossed our 50-yard line twice in the ballgame. They scored one touchdown against us, and they got the touchdown when we fumbled the center-quarterback exchange on our own 13-yard line. It's probably less than three inches of error, but that's what I'm going to give you, three inches. We also had five possessions against Colorado inside Colorado's 30-yard line with an opportunity to score. We missed a couple of field goal attempts by a few inches.

"We wanted to say to our players, 'This is how close you are as a football team to playing in the Orange Bowl. This is how close you are to being in a conference championship. Don't sell yourself short, because you've got to understand that you're good enough.'"

When Snyder was hired November 30, 1988, he made no promises about how many wins the Wildcats would get the following season. Nor did he say how fast improvement would come. People quizzed him on the numbers and he gave the same response. "I will not say how many victories we will have, or ever will have. I have no idea," he said at the press conference to announce his hiring. "I can't predict when. My only prediction is that it will happen. But I have no idea how long it will take. I just know it will get done."

And then, with a "let's suppose" attitude, he continued, "In the next year or two, we might win six. But we won't be there if we fall back down. What we're after is consistency."

The Cats did win six in the next two years, combined. Which made 1991 extremely important to Snyder in his own evaluation of the progress, just not in terms of numbers. "I don't deal in numbers of wins and losses," he said, looking back on the expectations he put on himself that season. "We don't have to be 7-4, we don't have to be 6-5. We don't have to be anything. Our goals are still the same. Our goals aren't going to change. Let's get better today. Let's be a better football team, a better person, today than we were yesterday, and let's do all the things that we can do to achieve that particular goal. Winning and losing takes care of itself after that."

Kansas State certainly had its share of luck in crossing the line. The turf at Kansas State was in desperate need of repair, but there was no money to repair it. Then alumni and boosters Dave and Carol Wagner of Dodge City, Kansas, won $35 million in the Kansas Lottery. They donated $800,000 and Kansas State had new turf. "I had been involved with Kansas State since 1960, when I started as a freshman," Dave Wagner said. "My wife and I had been active with the Catbackers, since we moved to Dodge City in 1979.

"With the lottery, we wanted to do something more and were in a position to do so. We met with Steve Miller and discussed the different areas in

Snyder didn't promise victories but he did promise his team would be competitive. Just ask this Colorado runner.

Brent Venables played middle linebacker for Kansas State in 1991 and '92 despite having a condition called super ventricular tachycardia – rapid heart beat syndrome. While it was not a life-threatening condition, it certainly made him the butt of a few jokes.

"I'd come to practice and I'd have a monitor on," he said. "There were all these cords and things stuck to my body, and they'd call me 'robo-backer' and 'heart attack.' Coach Snyder would say his garage door was malfunctioning at night, and ask if it was my monitor.

"To me the condition wasn't ever scary," he said, "because I had had it for years."

It is a sense of humor and his smile that strikes you first about Venables. He is not physically imposing, especially for a middle linebacker – "barely 6-feet on a good day,

which the athletic department was in need. There were four areas presented to us. Carol and I both felt that the turf was the area where we could impact the young men in the program. The pressbox was another area, but that wasn't for the kids. There were so many positive things that had been done, and this was just one more."

The season was one of personal highs and lows for Snyder. Besides the coaching honors he received, he was joined on the field by his son, Sean. Sean had redshirted at Iowa in 1988, when his father was still an assistant under Hayden Fry. After Coach Snyder left for Manhattan, Sean began his redshirt freshman year as the starter. But early in the season, he was benched and at the end of the 1989 season, he transfered to Kansas State. After sitting out the 1990 season, he took over the punting duties for his

playing at 203 pounds my entire career." He simply played his way onto the field and wouldn't let anybody take him off.

Venables had a chance to walk on at Kansas State right out of Salina South High School. The new coaching staff just had arrived and Venables didn't feel like he had received the type of attention he deserved. "When I left high school, I felt that I was a good enough player to come to Kansas State," he said. "At that time I was too bullheaded to come as a walk-on, and they didn't offer me a scholarship. So I told myself, 'I'm going to go to JuCo, and I'm never going to give Kansas or Kansas State another look.'"

He went to Garden City Community College, where he started for teams that went 9-2 and 10-1 in his two years. But with his team's games occurring on Saturday nights, he was able to listen to Kansas State's games in the afternoon. It frustrated him that nobody else on his team – those from Kansas or from out-of-state – showed any interest in how the Cats were playing. "I would tell them, 'Hey look, these guys are good,'" he said. "'I told you last year they were going to get better.'"

But his pleas for support fell on deaf ears, except his own. He suddenly regained his interest in giving K-State another try. He turned down full-ride offers to North Carolina State, Colorado State and New Mexico, as well as numerous I-AA schools. "Everybody in the world told me I was crazy to come to K-State as a walk-on," he said. "There was no need for linebackers in the program. They had 18. I feel fortunate that they accepted me as a walk-on.

"I wanted to be a part of this turn-around. I wanted to help put Kansas State on the map. I knew I couldn't do it by myself. I didn't think I would come in and be this huge impact player and take Kansas State to the Big Eight title, but I did want to be a part of the ground laying, help set the foundation."

Because he wasn't at K-State during the lean years, he felt like he cheated the guys who were. He was able to enjoy two years of success and then come in to the program when it was ready to "cross the line" to a winning season. "Brooks Barta, Chris Patterson, Michael Smith, Paul Watson, Russ Campbell – the guys who came here right away when it was at its worst – those guys are the ones who deserve to get the headlines," he said. "Those are the guys who had been here, who had been through it. They had believed in the coaching staff. They're the ones who went through the blood and the sweat and the tears together. I had absolutely no problem taking a back seat to those guys. They should be getting the credit, the limelight, the headlines, because they deserve it."

Venables' ability to deflect praise makes a good coaching attribute. Currently, he is a graduate assistant under Snyder, where he is learning the work ethic from a coaching standpoint. He is absorbing everything he can while he has the opportunity. "I always try to grasp everything possible that's around me," he said. "I always try to grab a perception of everything that's going on. Probably no one else would notice, but I would always watch what every coach is doing, especially Coach Snyder. I watch his demeanor, just how he goes about doing things. Then I watch other people and how they react."

It's that attention to detail that convinces Snyder that Venables will be a successful coach some day. "I think he'll be an excellent coach," Snyder said. "He could be excellent in a lot of things, whatever he chooses to do. He's a very intelligent young guy who understands how to get ahead, how to work for things."

Snyder, who learned a lot of his preparation as a graduate assistant at Southern California under John McKay, says he doesn't see himself in Venables, but others do. "He's probably way ahead of where I was at that age," Snyder said.

If he does become a head coach, it will be a dream come true, at least a recent one. "That's my lifetime goal, to be a head coach," he said. "I've always been an idealist. I was going to go to law school and be a big corporate lawyer, but after two years in this program, I decided I wanted to go into coaching."

You know he'll put his heart into it.

With so many off-the-field distractions, it was difficult for Snyder to keep his focus in 1991, but he was able to guide the Cats to a 7-4 season.

father's team in 1991.

But 1991 also saw some personal struggles for the KSU head coach. Early in the season, his mother, Marionetta, was diagnosed with a recurrence of cancer. Later in the season, his 97-year-old grandfather, George Owen, fell in his home. After he lay unconscious for hours, Snyder's daughter, Shannon, stopped by his house and found him on the floor. She called for an ambulance that took him to the hospital, where he remains.

"It was difficult," Snyder said. "I made sure I got to St. Joe (St. Joseph, Missouri – his home town where both his mother and grandfather lived) on a regular basis during the season. I would leave here late in the evening, spend the night, get up and see them in the morning, and then come back here in the afternoon for practice, meetings and preparation."

Then, in February 1992, his daughter, Meredith, was severely injured in an automobile accident in Dallas, and was rendered paralyzed from the neck down, with a very high spinal cord injury. The neurologist and the surgeon who attended her told her parents a couple of weeks after the accident that she never would walk again, that she would remain paralyzed from the neck down. Today she walks with the aid of a cane, drives her own automobile and has a great attitude.

"She's obviously made very remarkable progress from where we were at the time and what the prognosis initially was," Snyder said. "Last fall, I sent her to an institute in California. She was there for three and a half months with rehabilitation work that she hadn't done before. While she was there, her mother took her up to the mountains to ski. They put her on regular skis with a little bar attachment between

the toes of each ski so she wouldn't toe in, and put her on the bunny slope. She'd never been skiing before in her life. On the third day, she went down 10 or 12 times without falling...she really has come a long way."

Meredith has displayed some of that Snyder determination to the point where she has driven from her home in Dallas to Manhattan on several occasions. "She still has restrictions and still has a ways to go," her father says, "but she has made a miraculous recovery to this point."

But despite all the off-field problems, Bill Snyder's job is football coach. And he focused in on the field to help the Cats "cross the line."

The opener pitted the Wildcats against Indiana State, a Division I-AA team that finished 1990 at just 4-7. But the Wildcats played sporadically. They outgained the Sycamores by less than 100 yards, 384-308. But worse than that, the Wildcats allowed ISU to come back from 21-7 and 24-13 third-quarter deficits.

Indiana State took an early 7-0 lead when Von Ganoway returned an interception 32 yards for a touchdown. The Wildcats then ran off 21 unanswered points to open an apparently comfortable lead. But, after an ISU touchdown and a Tate Wright 41-yard field goal, Indiana State's Ray Allen connected with Charles Swann for a 78-yard TD strike to cut the Cats' lead to 24-19. In the fourth quarter, ISU went on a 75-yard drive and took the lead on another Allen-to-Swann touchdown pass with 3:24 remaining.

The Wildcats and their fans were harkening back to games in previous regimes when the team let wins get away as the Sycamores lined up for the extra point. But ahead only 25-24, Indiana State head coach Dennis Raetz decided to try for two points, to force the Cats to score a touchdown to earn a victory.

That's when William Price made history. "T," as he was called, picked off Allen's pass attempt in the end zone and raced 102 yards for the defensive extra points. It was the first time in the three-year history of an NCAA rule that allowed the defense to score two points on such a play that the game-winning points were achieved in that manner. It was only the fifth time the rule ever had been used in any Division I game.

"T. was encouraging us, 'Don't worry, we're going to be OK.' He was hooting and hollering," Jaime Mendez said. "T. was the type of guy who always downplayed the 14 goals and everything. He was the kind of guy who would say, 'Forget this. I don't worry about that. That's stupid.' But he bought in right then and there.

"He kind of picked up the whole defensive team. 'We can do this. We can win. We can win.' Everyone got on his shoulders, and he took us home. He came up with an interception the next play after they got the on-side kick. That had sort of deflated us again. He comes right out there and he's the cheerleader again. I thought to myself, 'This is unbelievable. I can't believe what I'm seeing here.' He sort of set the tone for that whole season with those two plays."

While Snyder was pleased to see Price buying into the program and subsequently lifting his team's spirits, he was not pleased with the total effort that night.

"What a great thing T. Price and our defense had done to put us in a position to win," Snyder said. "But after the score, our players all ran on the field and we were assessed a penalty on the ensuing kickoff. That really put us in jeopardy, because all they needed to do was to get themselves into field goal range and they would have a chip shot. By allowing them the additional field position, we certainly gave them that opportunity. When we went in the lockerroom, I was angry, I was upset with them. We had to be a football team that would learn to play, perform and react with poise.

When Andre Coleman eluded Matt Gay, he carried the winning touchdown into the end zone against Kansas.

"There were some lessons learned in that game. We found a way to lose it and we found a way to come back and win it. It made a real impact on the players. Ever since that day, every individual who was present for that ballgame, has a much truer, more specific understanding of that particular scenario, that you can't let up, you can't prepare indifferently. You've got to play them one at a time, and you've got to play each one as though they are the best team that you could possibly play against."

Snyder also was pleased with the atmosphere in the lockerroom following the game. Although safe in the assurance that they had won their season opener for the second straight year, the Wildcats were subdued. "Our players weren't too happy with the victory, not happy with the consistency," he said after the game. "I'm pleased about that. That tells me they've taken a step forward."

The Wildcats left no chance for any late-game comebacks in their second game against Idaho State, scoring on the opening possession and never looking back on the way to a 41-7 victory. Paul Watson scrambled in from the 4 to cap an 11-play, 71-yard drive. A Curtis Madden run and two Andre Coleman receptions lifted the Cats to a 27-0 lead before Idaho State got on the board. Tony Williams recovered a fumble in the end zone and J.J. Smith raced 72 yards for a touchdown on the first carry of his career.

The Wildcats continued to improve the following week as Northern Illinois ventured into Manhattan. This was a game of redemption for most of the Cats, since the Huskies had stopped Kansas State in each of the two previous seasons.

While the Cats doubled the Huskies, 34-17, Snyder

Erick Gallon rushed for 1,102 yards in 1991, the second-best season in school history.

had mixed feelings about the game. "We made mistakes," he said. "We want our kids to realize that you're not going to beat very many good football teams if you don't take better advantage of the opportunities you have. But by the same token, the joy of winning sometimes overshadows your performance."

Watson was 21 of 29 for 311 yards, but threw two interceptions, including one at the goal line with Kansas State up only 7-0 in the first half. Eric Gallon rushed for 106 yards, but fumbled at the NIU 29. The defense held Northern Illinois, a team that had rushed for 403 yards the previous year against them, to just 176 yards on the ground. But they also allowed the Huskies to convert seven of 12 third-down opportunities in the first half, including third-and-eight from their own 3 when Stacey McKinney hit Larry Wynn for a 65-yard gain.

The Cats owned the second half, outscoring NIU, 27-14, and they owned a 3-0 record heading into a match-up with eventual national champion Washington.

The Washington game was one Snyder did not want to play. He had tried to buy out the contract and trade it for a "winable" game, but the Huskies did not oblige. Faced with the prospect of squaring off against the nation's No. 4-ranked team – "the best college football team I've ever seen," said Holthus – Snyder was realistic.

Very few players can epitomize the Kansas State football program better than Paul Watson. He had to fight through seemingly insurmountable odds, many times over, finally to achieve his goal and be perceived as a champion.

Watson was one of the most highly recruited quarterbacks in the country after the fall of 1986, following a stellar career at Kansas City's Park Hill High School. He threw for more than 5,000 yards and 52 touchdowns in his varsity career, including setting a school record for yardage in his sophomore campaign.

Former Kansas State coach Stan Parrish touted Watson as the cornerstone of the future even before he took his first collegiate snap. Watson ate it up. "I was a very confident, cocky young man," he said. "I was really dumbfounded about what college ball was all about."

Watson redshirted in 1987, both to add bulk to his 6-2 frame (he came in at 175 pounds) and to "learn how the Big Eight actually worked," he said. "I needed to learn the system. That's why Coach Parrish had me travel to all the games. I went to every road game my freshman year, even though I wasn't going to play."

After a solid spring in 1988 and a good start to the fall camp, Watson was penciled in as the starter. Then the calamities started. Ten days before the season opener, the Cats were practicing the wishbone for their goal-line offense when Watson got hit. He dislocated his throwing shoulder, an injury that was pro-

jected to keep him from throwing the ball for six weeks. "It was a pretty dramatic letdown for me," he said. "But I had a good trainer who helped me through the rehab process. I was ready to play by the third week, but I didn't play against Tulane."

The following week, Watson finally made his collegiate debut in a home game against Louisiana Tech. It was quite a debut. On the first play from scrimmage, Watson crouched behind center Paul Yniguez, raised up and fired an 80-yard touchdown to David Brooks. Before the half ended, he had set a K-State record for touchdown passes in a game with four. He finished with 362 yards of passing and 364 yards of total offense, Big Eight highs for the season.

But the Tech game was a bitter disappointment for Watson and the Cats. The Bulldogs overcame a 28-7 halftime deficit to win, 31-28. Watson threw two interceptions in the fourth quarter that helped Tech's comeback. Following the game, Parrish announced that he would resign at the end of the season.

The next week against Missouri, Watson threw an interception on the final play of the first half. When he tried to tackle the defender, he reinjured his shoulder, putting him out for the season. "I ripped everything out of my shoulder," Watson said. "The whole shoulder came out of the socket."

When Bill Snyder arrived in December of 1988, one of his priorities was the quarterback position. He had

made a name for himself as the offensive coordinator and quarterbacks coach at Iowa, and he knew that an effective, strong quarterback was essential in the offense he was installing at K-State.

"When Coach Snyder came in, his first impression of Paul Watson was, basically, 'this kid will never play,'" Watson said. "I was going through rehab and I wasn't throwing that well. Before the surgery I had a really strong arm, but after the surgery I had lost 10 percent rotation. It was tough for me to throw deep, which was very critical in Coach Snyder's offense.

"Coach Snyder's point of view certainly was understandable."

Watson easily could have given up. But Snyder wouldn't let him. "Coach Snyder is a great motivator and a great coach," Watson said. "He has an A-1 staff who helps him. I don't take any credit away from him, but his staff and his players had a lot to do with it. As far as believing in Coach Snyder, I believe wholeheartedly in Coach Snyder, because he is a great person. He is a great football-minded person, and he knows how to get his kids motivated."

The biggest change, according to Watson, was in attitude. "When I was a freshman, the other team would score seven or 10 points, and we were over with, we were done. You might as well forget it." But Snyder would not allow that feeling to exist.

"In Coach Snyder's first year, we were trying our hardest to win," Watson

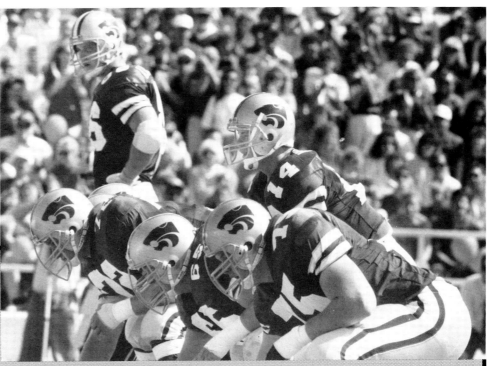

When asked if his 3-0 Cats were ready for the 2-0 Huskies, he said, "There is nobody ready for Washington." After the game, he hadn't changed his opinion at all. "From what I've seen, they're as good as any football team in the country right now," he said. "I think their defense is bet-

continued. "It wasn't one of the things that you knew you were going to win, we knew we weren't there yet, but we went out there and we busted our tails. Now you could see that everybody was giving their 100 percent. It wasn't that everybody was physically bigger and better and faster and quicker, it was the fact that everybody really concentrated on learning the system."

Watson battled for starting status through the next three years. He lost out to Carl Straw in 1989 and 1990, though he started four games in 1989 when Straw was hurt. Through three seasons, he had completed more than 50 percent of his passes for 1,651 yards. With Straw gone in 1991, Watson appeared to have a strong chance to regain his much-anticipated status as a starter.

But none of the quarterbacks in camp had a strong enough showing during training camp to be tabbed the starter. Watson finally was named the starter, but with the plan that he would be replaced in the second half each week. The plan worked fairly well for the Wildcats, as they went through the non-conference season at 3-1. The weekend before the Big Eight opener against Kansas, Watson was shot in the eye in a hunting accident, and again, it appeared that his chance would be erased. But Watson was not going to give up.

"A lot of people would have thrown the hat in and said, 'Forget it, I'm leaving,

I'm tired, I'm tired of working this hard. I don't want to overcome this,'" he said. "I've always been a sports lover, I always will be a sports lover, and I was brought up the way that you never quit unless you can't walk or throw the ball. Today, three years later, I go out and play ball and I won't quit unless somebody breaks my leg or breaks my arm. I'll do it until I can't do it anymore."

Watson started the KU game miserably. He threw an interception and fumbled three times in the first three quarters and was benched. But when the offense still couldn't move, Watson was put back in with the Cats down 12-3.

"I put Paul back in with the idea that he was a senior and he was more experienced," Snyder said. "This game, because he had been here longer, probably meant more to him and we hung our hat on him, and he did wonderful things. We talk about the drive at Oklahoma State with Chad May (in 1993), but certainly what Paul did is very comparable and maybe even surpasses that in the fact that he did it twice in back-to-back drives in the last eight to 12 minutes of the ballgame. It was very significant."

What Watson did in those last few minutes was drive the Wildcats to two

touchdowns and a 16-12 victory over Kansas. "There was no way we could lose that game," Watson said. "That was probably the worst first half of football I've ever played in my entire life. When I went back in, the team really backed me. Quentin (Neujahr) was a big part of my career. The guy always believed in me, every snap, every time something would happen, he knew I could do it. It was just a matter of doing it. He said during that game, 'Let's go, you can do it. Just calm down.' And Michael Smith and Frank Hernandez and Erick Gallon were all behind me. They said, 'Let's go now, let's do something.'"

Watson's confidence following that game enabled him to finish his career in outstanding fashion. He earned second-team all-Big Eight honors from the coaches after leading the conference in total offense with 214 yards per game.

"That game was a real mark of his fortitude and the quality of his character," Snyder said. "His confidence shot up. Everybody's confidence in him elevated immensely. It was a proud moment.

"That was a special moment in his life and a special moment in Kansas State history."

ter than their offense, but they're solid on both sides of the ball."

The Huskies had three future NFL first-round draft picks (defensive lineman Steve Emtman [No. 1 overall], wide receiver Mario Bailey and defensive back Dana Hall).

While the final score may not indicate it, the Wildcats gained confidence, despite the 56-3 final. The Huskies had scored twice less than five minutes into the game and held a 35-3 halftime lead. The offense was balanced, gaining 240 yards through the air, two more than on the ground. The Cats managed minus-17 rushing for the game. Yet there were positives.

Watson was 17 for 23 for 232 yards against arguably the best defense in the country. He threw 12 of his completions to Michael Smith for 174 yards, giving Smith the Kansas State career yardage mark with 2,032.

"That team was nothing less than awesome," Watson said. "But we proved that we could throw the ball against anybody."

Washington's quarterback Billy Joe Hobert called the Cats "a pretty competitive team. They picked a pretty bad day to play us. Everything clicked."

Don James, the veteran Huskies coach noted at the end of the season that Kansas State was "the most prepared to play" of any team the Huskies had faced in their national championship season.

Sideline celebrations have become a regular occurrence under Snyder.

Chris Patterson (opposite page) showed KU's Tony Sands that crossing the line against K-State's defense was not going to be easy.

"We got our tails whacked," Snyder said. "But I think because the offense got some yardage, and moved the ball a little bit between the 30s that there was a ray of hope that we had some ability offensively to move the ball. Had we gotten beat as badly against Washington as we did, and not won ballgames prior to that, then that would have been somewhat of a damaging scenario, because it wouldn't have been just one ballgame, but it could have directed the outcome of the next few ballgames."

Fresh off their second straight 3-1 non-conference season, the Wildcats opened the Big Eight season with a grudge match against cross-state rival Kansas. It was more than just another KU-K-State game. Both teams entered the game with 3-1 records and a solid chance for a winning record. The last time the Cats had won more than they lost was 1982, one year after the Jayhawks' last plus-.500 year. The winner also would have the inside track for a first division finish in the Big Eight.

But, for reasons not known to many fans, the game held even more significance for Kansas State. Five-year old James Owens was in the final weeks of his life as he was suffering from leukemia. The Cats had adopted James as one of their own, visiting him and taking him gifts. He attended his first college football game to watch the Cats and the Jayhawks do battle, and Michael Smith told James during a visit to a practice that week that the team was dedicating this Homecoming game to him.

James and more than 40,000 of his friends enjoyed this one.

It may be easy to pick Watson as the hero on this day. It may even be correct. He engineered two touchdown drives in the fourth quarter to lift the Wildcats to a 16-12 victory. But the game was won by the defense. Several times.

The Wildcats fell behind 12-3, and looked to be out of it when KU had first-and-10 at the KSU 15 with less than 10 minutes left in the fourth quarter. Three running plays netted KU nine yards, setting up fourth-and-one. K-State already had stopped two fourth-and-one situations when the Jayhawks tried running, so KU went to the air. Kenny Drayton got open in the end zone, but Chip Hilleary overthrew him.

Watson, then got another chance. He had been eight of 21 up to that point and had been pulled from the lineup, but after his backup could fare no better, he came back in the game. "There was no way we were going to lose that game," Watson said.

"That's probably the worst first half of football I had played in my life. I stunk. I had no complaints about being taken out. But when my replacement started having trouble, I was on the phone with Coach (Del) Miller in the pressbox. The big decision was whether to put me back in or not.

"I told Coach Miller that I could do it. I said, 'Don't be afraid to put me back in.'"

Snyder was more succinct. "It was obvious that the other guy wasn't going to do it and I put Paul back in with the idea that he was a senior and he was more experienced," the coach said. "This game, because he had been here longer, probably meant more to him. We hung our hat on him, and he did wonderful things. We talk about the drive at Oklahoma State with Chad May, but certainly what Paul did is very comparable and maybe even surpasses that in the fact that he did it twice in back-to-back drives in the last eight to 12 minutes of the ballgame."

Watson took over the KSU offense at his own 6. He completed eight passes in 11 attempts to take the Cats to the KU 10. Eric Gallon then ran in to bring the Cats to within two points.

Two ticks past the 4:00 mark, Snyder had to choose whether to try an on-side kick. He decided against it because of the confidence of his defensive coaches. "The thought went through my mind to on-side kick it," he said. "But I went to our defensive coaches and said, 'You just tell me if you think you can get us three and out (forcing them to punt).' And by golly, they said they could and they did it. That's why I chose not to on-side kick."

"I think we built confidence in the coaches going into the fourth quarter," linebacker Joe Boone said. "There was something in the air that day that you could look into the eyes of every defensive player and they were saying, 'I'm not lying down. I'm not doing anything other than giving it my best shot.'"

Following the KU punt, the Cats took over on their 34. After a 12-yard gain, they lost two yards on the next two plays, setting up third-and-12. But Watson hit Russ Campbell for a 22-yard gain to the KU 34. A first-down pass was incomplete. On second down, Watson was flushed from the pocket. Just before running out of bounds, he spotted Andre Coleman open at the 15. He lofted the ball down field where Coleman hauled it in. Coleman sidestepped the defender and stepped into the end zone to give KSU the lead. The Cats tried for two, but missed.

The Cats had struck so quickly, however, they left Kansas with 1:58 on the clock. The defense was called upon one more time to hold. "The coaches told us we were a fire department and we had to put out the fires," linebacker Brooks Barta said of the defensive effort on the day.

After an emotional win against the Jayhawks, seniors Paul Watson and Michael Smith embrace their first victory over KU.

Things got hot in the final seconds. Kansas drove to the Kansas State 10-yard line, but ran out of time. A pass into the end zone was deflected by Rogerick Green, and would not have counted anyway, since the clock expired before the play started.

"That was probably the ultimate feeling in college football, to come from behind like that and have such a great defensive game as a total defense," Barta recalled. "To come back and score in the last two minutes, I just remember the elation after that game. I remember the family, the friends, the players, everybody was just on an incredible high."

For in-state kids like Barta and Brent Venables, the game was extra special. "That was the game that brought it all together for me," Venables said. "To me, it was a dream to be able to come in there and make the big play to beat them, or just to be a part of that. I knew that was a huge, huge rivalry.

"I was really, really frustrated because I wasn't playing much. I asked Coach Snyder, 'What do I have to do to play?' He said, 'You've got to get in better shape. Run stairs.' So I started running stairs after practice. I was going to do everything I could. I

Quentin Neujahr is one great big Surprise. There. It's been said.

Neujahr came to Kansas State from *Surprise*, Nebraska, where he grew up a Nebraska Cornhuskers fan. "Nebraska actively recruited me," he said. "Every weekend during the high school season I'd go to Lincoln. We'd play our games on Friday and I'd go to a college football game on Saturday. They'd take me up there and they'd treat me like a king. They'd show you around and say, 'This could be you, this could be your jersey. You could wear the scarlet and gray.'

"If they had never really recruited me at all, I wouldn't have thought anything about it. But once somebody starts recruiting you and says, 'You're a great athlete, we want you to come here,' it grabs your attention. When it came time to offer me a scholarship, they said, 'We're going to take this kid out of Colorado instead of you, because we feel maybe you'll walk on. It's hard to get players from out-of-state to walk on. He's going to come in at the same level you are. We want to make him the center; you're a center. You can compete with him. After your third year, maybe you can play.'"

Neujahr knew that his chances at Nebraska were not good. It would be difficult to supplant a scholarship player. So he was left with the choice of accepting a scholarship offer from Kansas State or a late offer from the University of Wyoming. His choice of Kansas State had less to do with the fact that he believed Bill Snyder could turn around the worst program in the conference, than it did with his loyalty.

"Wyoming had offered me a scholarship the day before the signing date," he said. "I was kind of on their C or D or Z list. I wasn't going to get offered a scholarship until they said, 'If we can't get anybody else, we'll take you.' I was kind of second fiddle in the band. My decision then was deciding between a 27-game (winless) streak and playing in the Big Eight, or going to the back-to-back WAC champions. I asked my high school wrestling coach which I should choose. He said, 'Kansas State isn't very appealing, but you gave them your word and your word is more important than anything else you could ever have.'"

Surprise, Neujahr was a Wildcat.

Neujahr was an undersized center when he started his career at K-State. "Quentin came from a program that could not help him to develop a great deal physically," Snyder said. "They didn't have the weight facilities to gain a great deal of strength. Even though he was sizable, he came to us a long way away from where most youngsters are in terms of strength and physical attributes.

"He had to work extremely hard in the weight room as well as on the field. It took him a considerable amount of time to gain the kind of strength that he needed, and yet he was able to circumvent that particular weakness quite well. I think most of it was because he studied the game diligently. He made very good decisions. He was not prone to making mental mistakes on the field. It's hard to find a freshman who is able to do that, but he certainly was. He got better all the time."

Despite being undersized – "I wasn't ready for the Big Eight," he said – he started the first game of his redshirt freshman year. And the next one. And everyone after that until he had started 45 consecutive games, a school record. He finished his career as a third-team all-America, as selected by the NFL Draft Report. He now is vying for a spot on an NFL roster. Quite a Surprise for someone who slipped out from under the noses of the Cornhuskers.

But Neujahr doesn't take his rise to prominence too seriously. He says his consecutive-games-started streak was not because of his skill or the fact that he impressed Snyder with his work ethic. "I was the only center on the roster," he joked. "That had a lot to

camped out in Coach (Jim) Leavitt's office watching all the Kansas video tape I could. The better you know your opponent, the more successful you're going to be. I spent the week doing extra lifting or watching film."

It was an approach that was shared by all the Cats for the biggest game in their collective careers. And it paid off. Kansas State was in first place heading into the game at Nebraska. There, the Cats played like a title contender.

The teams went into the half tied at 17-17 as Watson hit Smith for two first-half TDs. The Cats took a 24-17 lead in the third quarter when C.J. Masters scooped up a

do with it."

And he refuses to gloat about proving the skeptics wrong until he makes that NFL roster and becomes a star. "I've proven some things that I wanted to prove," he said, "but I'm not done yet. I've got to take it to another level. I've got to be able to say, 'I could play in the Big Eight and I can play in a league above your league. I can do anything that you say I can't.'"

Being from a small town, Neujahr often was accused of being naive. But that is not true. "I don't always see everything that's being pulled down over my head," he said. "But I'm pretty aware of what goes on and what it takes to be successful. I'm not going to do anything halfway."

It's that attitude that made it difficult to stay at Kansas State. Part way through his freshman year, he considered leaving. The Cats had lost their first three and things did not look promising. But he never quit anything in his life, and he wasn't about to start here.

Still, well into his third year at Kansas State, he was receiving letters from friends back home, saying it was not too late to walk away from a losing program and come back to Nebraska. "It didn't stop after the first year," Neujahr said. "It was the second and the third years and people were saying, 'Don't go down with this sinking ship. You're in way over your head and nothing is going to happen there.' It takes a lot of discipline and it takes a lot of courage to say, 'I started something and I'm not going to walk away from it.'"

So Neujahr stayed at Kansas State. He never got to experience a victory against Nebraska, something that still eats at him. But the final game of his career was a win against Wyoming, the other school that only gave him a cursory look.

But, more amazingly, Neujahr had been part of a bowl victory at Kansas State. He had been an integral part of the greatest turnaround in college football history.

No Surprise there.

Eric Gallon and the Cats found it tough going against the Buffs, spoiling a stellar effort by the **KSU** defense.

Lance Lewis fumble and ran 40 yards for the score. Nebraska responded with a nine-play, 67-yard drive to tie the score on Johnny Mitchell's 4-yard catch.

Kansas State wouldn't quit. Keyed by a 34-yard completion to Smith, Watson led the Cats on a 79-yard drive in eight plays. Watson scored the touchdown himself on a 3-yard keeper. Following a Nebraska punt, the Wildcats were in business to put the game nearly out of reach.

The Cats had the ball at the NU 16 on a third-and-two play. Eric Gallon had clear sailing to a first down and maybe a score, when he slipped on the wet turf. Fourth down provided Tate Wright with a 32-yard field goal attempt that sailed just left. Wright and Watson, the holder, thought it was good, but the momentum slipped away with the errant kick.

Nebraska scored two touchdowns in a 4:02 spread to take a 38-31 lead with 2:47 left. But even then, the Wildcats did not quit. They moved the ball from their own 27 to the Nebraska 11 with just under a minute remaining. Madden gained 4 yards on first down. Watson then threw two incomplete passes, including one to Smith in the end zone.

Finally, on fourth-and-six from the 7, Watson tried to hit Russ Campbell, but Trev Alberts jarred the ball lose and the No. 9-ranked Huskers had held on.

"When they scored the last one, there was very little time remaining," Snyder said. "As we got together on the sideline – Paul, Michael, the rest of our offense – our discussion was that we were going to go for two points. We skipped over the idea that we might not score. That's what I really appreciated about these guys and how far they had come.

"I think the Kansas ballgame was instrumental in that – there wasn't any doubt in their minds. They knew that wherever they got the kickoff, they were going to move the ball down the field and they were going to score. The only concern on the sideline was whether we were going to kick the extra point or go for two. We were going to play for the win. It wasn't just me. It was the players. Then we directed our focus toward moving down the field and what needed to be done."

The Wildcats could blame neither the officials nor an opponent's potent offensive attack in their next loss, a 10-0 stinker at home to Colorado. They only could blame themselves. In a switch from the previous week, the defense carried the offense.

The defense had what Snyder called the finest defensive effort he had seen in his three years at Kansas State, holding the defending national champions to 10 points and 339 yards of total offense, nearly 300 fewer than the previous year. The Buffaloes' only touch-down drive came after Watson fumbled a snap and CU recovered at the KSU 13.

In the first half, the Cats had a first down inside the CU 25-yard line four times without scoring. Two of the drives ended in interceptions and the other two in missed field goals. The second half was worse. The Cats only ventured into CU territory one time and fumbled the ball on the play.

The Cats were warmed by the feeling they played another Top-20 team nose-to-nose, but moral victories were starting to become painful losses. "I know that nobody was satisfied that we lost 10-0 to Colorado and 38-31 to Nebraska, definitely both winable games," Michael Smith recalled. "Coming off the field against Nebraska, that was the sickest feeling in the world to hear those people cheering for us. They were sympathizing for us, because we played so well but we still lost. I usually get along with the media, but that day I was so sick to my stomach I didn't want to talk to anybody, because I knew that we should have won that game."

Beginning in 1991, the NCAA required Division I-A teams to win six games against other I-A opponents in order to be eligible to compete in a bowl game. Considering the Wildcats' four wins included victories against Indiana State and Idaho State, members of the NCAA's Division I-AA, the only way the Cats could win six I-A games was by defeating Oklahoma in Norman. They then would have to win their next three and complete an 8-3 season.

Oklahoma saw to it that KSU's bowl plans were disintegrated. Storming to a 21-0 lead early in the second quarter, the Sooners cruised to a 28-7 win. While the Cats spoke with the NCAA to see if the six-win rule could be waived, since one of the games (Indiana State) had been scheduled before the rule was instituted, the NCAA Special Events Committee rejected the appeal and the Cats had to be satisfied with trying for the three-game sweep to close a 7-4 season.

Looking back, Snyder is not so sure that going to a bowl game following the 1991 season would have been the best thing for the program.

"I didn't want it to be a program of shortcuts. That doesn't mean I didn't want us to go to a bowl game," he said. "If we were legitimately to be perceived as a bowl team, then that's what our players deserved and I wanted them to go. Our philosophy had always been that we wanted to build this program on solid ground and we didn't want to take shortcuts. Shortcuts will normally come back to haunt you."

Still, Snyder tried to get the six-win rule waived because he believed in his coaches and players, and above all had great compassion for his seniors. He held out hope that the Cats could receive an invitation, even if it wasn't waived. "I've been around the game for a long time, and the rules around bowl game selections have been violated from day one. So my sensitivity to it was that the bowl committees were the ones who would make the decisions on whom they wanted and whom they didn't want. I wouldn't bet the house on it, but it was my feeling that they might bypass that particular NCAA regulation and select whomever they wanted if they were good enough to go. The idea of litigation was pursued, but I wasn't interested in a legal battle. I only wanted us to have an opportunity to participate in a bowl game if there were a bowl that was interested in us, which I believe wasn't the case."

Holthus felt a range of emotions. "There was a little bit of selfish disappointment because I wanted finally to go to a bowl game," he said. "But I also felt disappointment for the seniors – Michael Smith, Frank Hernandez, Paul Watson, Russ Campbell – those people who had been a part of this since 1988. They signed with Kansas State prior to Coach Snyder being here, buying into his philosophy and turning this thing around. I almost wish that 30 years from now, or in Heaven or something, they'll get a chance to go to a bowl. Those guys deserve one."

With nothing to play for but a lot of pride, the Wildcats sought to end another long losing streak. This was a 30-game Big Eight road losing streak, and the Iowa State Cyclones stood in the way. It wasn't so important who stood out for the Cats; the domination was complete in a 37-7 victory.

There was balance on offense – 231 yards on the ground and 209 through the air. The defense held Iowa State to 142 yards of total offense after the first quarter, 70 after intermission. Smith tied a KSU record by catching three touchdowns.

"Kansas State just has a better group of players to play with," Iowa State coach Jim Walden said.

The 30-point victory was the largest margin of victory on the road since 1955 when the Cats skunked Kansas, 46-0. "I guess 30 must be the magic number," Watson said.

"Cross the line" was the team slogan for the Wildcats in 1991. But never was it more appropriate than it was against Missouri in the 10th game. The Tigers came in with a potent offense, led by quarterback Phil Johnson. They had the reputation that they could score on anybody.

Not in this Cat-fight.

The Cats dominated every phase of the game in a 32-0 defeat of the Tigers. Not only did the Cats assure themselves of a winning season for only the second time since 1970, ironically the last time they shut out a Big Eight opponent, but the Cats did not allow the Tigers to cross the line – the Cats' 35-yard line.

"Our players always have been great about accepting challenges," Snyder said. "They had a chance to leave their signature on a job well done against a real quality offense."

It would be hard to pick a single Cat to decorate as the player of the game. Eric Gallon rushed for 184 yards, the second most ever against a Big Eight opponent. The defense held Mizzou to 260 total yards and caused 11 fumbles, six of which were recovered by the Wildcats. "We were hittin' and every time you saw the ball on the ground there were four or five K-Staters around the ball," defensive end Elijah Alexander said.

The offense, meanwhile, had little trouble negotiating the slick turf for 492 yards.

It marked the first time that K-State had won consecutive games by 30 points or more since 1917, when the competition was Washburn and Washington University of St. Louis.

It was particularly meaningful to the seniors, who not only experienced a winning season for the first time, but closed the home portion of their careers on a resounding note. After the game, Watson, a native of Missouri, and tight end Al Jones ran to the bell at the north end of the field and rang it six times. "It couldn't feel any better than to do it after beating Missouri," Watson said.

It also felt pretty good, since Missouri coach Bob Stull had questioned the improvement the Wildcats had shown and said only a match-up on game day really would prove the turnaround. He changed his tune after the game, saying, "They are playing with a lot of confidence now and they are a very good football team."

The Cats closed the 1991 season with a nondescript 36-26 win at Oklahoma State. The fact that a conference road win was not big news and that Kansas State could play "iffy" and still win comfortably showed just how much progress had been made.

"The big factor there was winning in the conference on the road, and just winning on the road period," Snyder said. "I'd never really stressed with players that we hadn't won on the road; we've got to win on the road. I'd never done that because we try to build up the feeling that we're going to play well on any field. We can't make a tremendous distinction between playing at home and going some place else to play. Then we're setting ourselves up for failure when we travel. So we don't put a lot of emphasis on that. It's just a matter of knowing that wherever you are, whether it's here or any place else, if you play as well as you can, you've got a chance to win.

The Cats did not allow Missouri any room to breathe, posting their first shut out over a Big Eight opponent since 1970.

"In retrospect you can go back and look at it and say that you cleared the hurdle. You've taken another stride."

A few Wildcats had stellar days against Oklahoma State, including senior tight end Russ Campbell. He caught eight passes for 169 yards. Both were career highs, with the 169 yards standing as the sixth-best yardage day in school history. It also allowed him to join Smith and Hernandez as career 1,000-yard receivers, which made K-State the first Big Eight school to have three receivers with that many career yards on the same team.

Eric Gallon had his third 175-yard-plus game of the season (he had two days of 184 yards), which gave him three of the top eight rushing yardage days in school history. His 1,102 yards made him the third Wildcat to gain 1,000 yards in a season. Kicker Tate Wright tied a school record with three field goals in a game, significant because Wright hailed from Stillwater.

With the possibility of a bowl game out of the picture, the Cats had to be satisfied with a 7-4 season. And though there was disappointment the season was over, there was satisfaction in a job well done.

"I'm happy with the win; 7-4 is just fine," Snyder said. "We'd like to be playing a 12th ballgame, but we're all tired. It's been a long, hard season. We've made progress."

1992
DEFENSE, SPECIAL TEAMS AND A BLOCK PARTY

If 1991 was the season in which the Kansas State Wildcats "crossed the line," then 1992 was when the Wildcats were knocked off-line. The Cats learned lessons about skipping hurdles, high expectations and not taking anything for granted.

"I didn't have a goal for 1992, except to improve every day," Coach Bill Snyder said. "That particular goal went down before we went up. I think there was a time in the season where that took hold, the latter part of the season. It was a difficult season. We were all disappointed in the outcome of the season, and yet I was proud of a lot of our youngsters and our coaches, because under duress and under difficult times, they redoubled their efforts and got us back on track, and performed well enough to come back and finish the season on a rather positive note.

"I think the '93 season indicated that we realized the error of our ways."

It was easy for the 1992 Cats to be confident. They had come off the best season in nearly 40 years and were one NCAA regulation short of appearing in a bowl game for the second time in school history. They returned 16 starters from that team, including first-team all-conference defenders Jaime Mendez and Brooks Barta. They were under

Gallon's numbers (22 carries for 87 yards) in the first game were impressive, especially since he wasn't even supposed to be ready to play.

Mendez' four interceptions helped the Cats dispose of the Owls.

the leadership of Snyder, the third coach in Big Eight history to garner Coach of the Year honors in back-to-back seasons (Nebraska's Bob Devaney and Oklahoma's Barry Switzer are the others).

One of The Wildcat's Fourteen Goals for Success is to "Improve every day – as a player, person and student." That also is a goal of the program. A slight improvement from the previous year and the 1992 Wildcats would be bowling during the postseason.

But there were big question marks heading into the season. Not unlike years past, there was a quarterback controversy. There was no experience at the position and neither of the top candidates seized the opportunity. With nearly 60 percent of their offense coming through the passing game the previous year, much was expected from the position.

The running game was a question mark, too, with second-team all-Big Eight running back Eric Gallon trying to return from a major knee injury suffered during spring practice. Gallon had recorded the second-best rushing total in school history (1,161 yards – nearly 1,000 yards better than the next best total by a running back in 1991), but until he stepped on the field, there would be questions about his ability to recover.

Unfortunately, the question marks ruled. The offense never got untracked, though there were games when it was respectable. The 1992 season was carried by the defense and the special teams.

The Cats opened the season with a 27-12 victory over Montana that would be a good predictor of the season to come. The defense held the Grizzlies to minus-1 yard rushing while the offense was sporadic. The Wildcats quarterbacks combined for 219 yards but on just seven completions in 25 attempts.

The bright spot on offense was Gallon. When he injured his knee in mid-April, optimistic reports were for a mid-October return. A more likely scenario would be no senior season. But when starter J. J. Smith twisted his ankle on the second play from scrimmage, Gallon trotted on to the field. He finished with 87 yards on 22 carries.

"I really didn't know what my first game back would be like," Gallon said. "I just knew that whenever I played, I wanted to run as hard as I ever did before. Coach Snyder and I talked about my playing time being limited to 15 or 20 snaps, but I ended up playing about 55."

The following week, the Cats rose to the occasion once again, though it might be more accurate to say that Mendez rose to the occasion. Mendez picked off four passes against Temple as the Cats shut down the Owls, 35-14.

The Cats raced to a 28-0 lead at halftime, behind three of Mendez's interceptions and four short running plays. Gallon had 98 of his game-high 134 yards rushing (a total that would earn him Big Eight Offensive Player of the Week honors) before intermission. And Brent Venables recorded seven of his 13 tackles before the band played.

But inconsistency haunted the Cats in the second half. Temple had touchdown drives of 68 and 80 yards to cut the lead to 28-14 with nearly a full quarter remaining. The Owls held the Cats to 23 yards of offense in the third quarter.

But Mendez's fourth interception stopped Temple and led to a sustained, 75-yard drive that iced the game.

"We just didn't show the experience and maturity to come back and perform as well in the second half," Snyder said following the contest. It was a theme that would be repeated too often for Snyder's tastes in 1992.

A third straight 15-point-plus margin of victory still did not get the Cats out of the doldrums. The victim was New Mexico State, which came into the game at 3-1 and averaging 32 points per game. But following the Wildcats' 19-0 victory, the mood in the KSU lockerroom was downright angry. "We expect to play better than that," Mendez said of the defense.

The offense ended up with decent numbers, outgaining New Mexico State, 355 to 230, but it was inconsistent to the point where Snyder described it as "somewhere between bad and whatever the next level down was."

The Cats had started 3-0 for the second straight season, but Snyder knew they were not playing to the level of which they were capable. "They probably were ugly wins," he said looking back. "We didn't play like I wanted us to. We just weren't in sync. We were missing something here and something there. There wasn't continuity with this group at that point. I knew that even though we were winning, there can be good and bad in winning. There was some bad involved in winning early that season and that was that it was adding to that false sense of security.

"That's kind of the essence of the global picture, the five-year period. When you take young guys who are somewhere between 17 and 22 years old, you can relate very easily to the theory that somewhere along the line you learn about not putting your hand on the stove after you've done so before. It's the learning experiences in life that allow us to grow."

The first hot stove was a University of Kansas team that may have been the Jayhawks' best in more than 20 years. (Because of a schedule change, the Cats' fourth non-conference game was into the Big Eight season. Before a trip to Logan, Utah, to play Utah State, the Wildcats traveled the 90 miles down Interstate 70 to square off with the Jayhawks.) It was the start of a four-game road stretch where the Wildcats went from struggling winners to just plain struggling.

Twenty. That's the number of Kansas State plays – out of 54 – that resulted in lost yardage against Kansas. Of the Cats' first nine plays, eight resulted in lost yardage or a turnover, even though Kansas couldn't convert the opportunities into points.

It hardly mattered that Kansas' offense sputtered slightly. The Wildcats could not muster a first down during the first half. Their only points came on C.J. Masters' 80-yard interception return for a touchdown. Kansas outgained the Wildcats, 451-69, including holding the Cats to minus-56 yards rushing, 239 below their average.

"That's the best defensive football team that we've played against since I've been at K-State," Snyder said after the game. "Their front four was awesome and they just didn't give us any room to operate." That defense sacked the Wildcats QB nine times.

"I don't know how much worse it could have been," the coach recalled two years later. "Maybe we thought we were a little better than we really were at the time. Our players had come off of three wins, so our guys thought they were on a roll. There wasn't a fear going down there, but unfortunately there was not the respect that needed to be there either. Consequently, it was a devastating game.

"They were better prepared than we were."

If any game in the 1992 season epitomized the entire year, it was the next game against Utah State. The game looked like a good opportunity to rebound following the loss to Kansas. Utah State had not won a non-conference game in five seasons and had

Brooks Barta remembers the first time he met Bob Cope, the defensive coordinator under first-year coach Bill Snyder in 1989. "I introduced myself and he kind of looked past me," Barta said. "He had a look like, 'I don't know who this guy is.' I was 190 pounds at the time and didn't fit the image of a college football player."

Barta always has battled misconceptions about his ability to play middle linebacker because of his size. Even at the end of his five-year career at K-State, he packed just 220 pounds on his 6-foot frame. "That's something I tried to share with some of the younger players coming into the program," Barta said. "There were a lot of us out there who didn't come from highly recruited backgrounds. But we went out and worked each and every day and tried to become better players.

"You can go to the chalk board and draw up all the qualities for a Big Eight linebacker, and I didn't fit too many of those qualities."

But as the old saying goes, you can't measure the size of a man's heart.

Barta's probably was big enough to stretch the number 44 on his purple jersey. He recorded 19 tackles in the third game of his freshman year. He became the only player to lead K-State in tackles for four straight years and finished his career as the second-leading tackler in school history and the 10th in Big Eight Conference history.

Barta has been around football since he was 7 or 8 years old. His father, Roger, has been the high school football coach at Smith Center, Kansas, since 1978. "I was always around practice," he said. "I was always in the coaches meeting. I was always watching film with my dad. Those are some of my fondest memories. At 11:30 Saturday night, we would be sitting down watching the old super-8 films on the wall in the basement." As the assistant football coach at Abilene High School, he still does that.

"Growing up around football, I think over time I developed a feeling and a sense for the game," he said. "There were some things that were in me that allowed me to be a pretty good football

player and see and understand some things that a lot of people don't understand. That helped me cut some corners."

Mitch Holthus, the "Voice of the Wildcats" who also grew up in Smith Center, calls Barta, "a trademark player of the program since Coach Snyder arrived. Here's a guy who was told he wasn't big enough or fast enough, and he became the 10th all-time leading tackler in the history of the conference. Being from the same home town, I've always respected the way he approached the game, his work ethic as a player and the way he represented the program. He was the prototype Bill Snyder player. For a kid like that to come from where I grew up just made it all the better."

Snyder gets a little miffed when people call Barta undersized. He notes that other players played the position at Barta's size or smaller. "He may have been by other people's standards, but not ours," Snyder said. "Brooks just got more out of himself than most people do.

won only once in five games in 1992. Make that twice.

The Aggies scored their first touchdown after Sean Snyder's punt was blocked and recovered at the KSU 9. Three plays later, Abu Wilson scored from the 3. Gallon ran six times for 44 yards on the Cats' next drive, leading to a 3-yard quarterback plunge, tying the game at 7-7.

Then the Aggies scored 21 unanswered points. Following two field goals that gave Utah State a 13-7 halftime lead, the Aggies scored on two long interception returns on consecutive KSU possessions. One followed a quarterback sack when the ball floated into Dave Balls' hands and he rum-

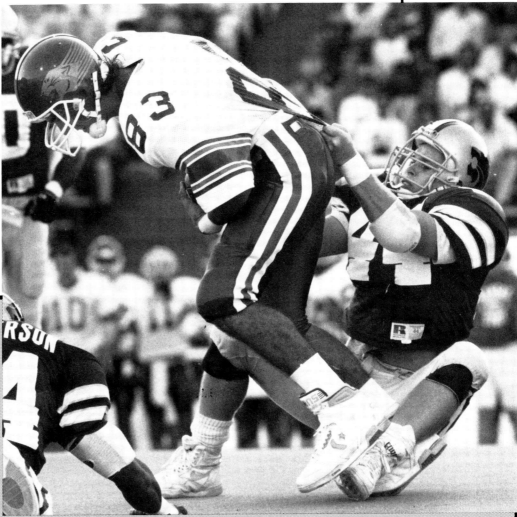

"He always felt that he was in the game by a process of elimination, but I don't see it that way. We always felt that Brooks was a good player and would continue to get better because of his work ethic. He deserved to be the guy who was on the field for all those years. It wasn't because there weren't other guys around. As the years went on, we had better players. Had he not been the quality of player that he was, someone else would have stepped in and played."

The same was true at Smith Center, where Barta was the lone linebacker in a 6-1 defense. He was expected to make the plays. On offense, he teamed with future K-Stater Jeff Simoneau to rush for more than 3,500 yards during their junior year, when they led the Redmen to the

Kansas Class 3A championship. An upset loss in the district playoffs kept them from going for a repeat championship their senior year.

Yet when it came time for him to move to the next level, he only received cursory interest. Kansas State was one of four Division I-A schools that offered him an opportunity. Wyoming and Air Force of the Western Athletic Conference joined Kansas and K-State. He wanted to stay close to home.

"I wanted my father to get a chance to come and see me play," he said. "For some reason, I think I just had a gut

feeling that K-State was due. I felt real comfortable at Kansas State as a university itself. There was a player from my high school who had played at KU. His experiences weren't great there. I think K-State was just the right place for me."

And after leading K-State in tackles for four years, it was obvious that Brooks Barta was right where he belonged. "Brooks is as much a K-Stater as anyone I've known," Snyder said. "He truly is a wonderful young man. He always will be very special to us."

bled 50 yards for the score. Then, back-up quarterback Matt Garber tried to throw the ball out of bounds, but it was picked by Jermaine Younger, who ran it back 59 yards.

The Cats got to within 12 when Garber scored from the 8 and Kenny McEntyre tackled punter Doug Beach in the end zone for a safety. But the final eight minutes provided no offensive threats for K-State.

"We hadn't made that continual improvement through that part of the season," Snyder said. "It wasn't all the players. We, as coaches, contributed to that as well. We made a few changes and they didn't work out as we had anticipated.

"The Utah State game was disappointing for everybody and perhaps more disappointing than any. Our players were very emotional after the ballgame in regard to the loss. Now all of a sudden they sensed that a downward spiral had begun. They could rationalize and probably tried to in their own minds that against Kansas they didn't play well. Kansas was pretty good. Consequently, they were still letting themselves in for a very rude awakening which certainly took place at Utah State."

"The feeling I had coming home from Utah State was one of the worst feelings I have ever had," Holthus said.

The loss to Kansas was disappointing because the offense was ineffective and it was against the Wildcats' biggest rival. The loss to Utah State was disappointing because the Cats let a weaker team dictate the game. But the loss to Colorado the next week was as total as the Cats had suffered under Snyder since his first season in Manhattan.

The Kansas State offense was shut out for the second time in three weeks, gaining just 16 yards of total offense. That broke the Big Eight record for fewest yards gained in a conference game, breaking the old mark of 31 by Nebraska against Colorado in 1961. On the ground, the Cats lost 24 yards on 24 carries. That gave them a three-game average of minus-5.3 yards.

Fifteen of the Wildcats' 17 possessions ended with only three plays.

Not to be outdone, the defense gave up 54 points and 514 yards.

"Outside of punting, there wasn't anything we did very well," Snyder said. "Offensively we laid eggs and defensively we were on the field too much."

"This team had kind of forgotten where it came from," Barta said. "This was a team

One-time walk-on Matt Garber (12) finished his career as the starter while Chad May (5) only could watch from the sidelines during his redshirt year.

that had to scratch and claw and fight. We had to outplay people. We still weren't to the point where we had better athletes than other people had."

It was a frustrating time for Snyder and the Cats, because they had fallen short of Goal No. 2 – Improve Every Day. This team seemed to be getting worse instead of better. "There was tension in the lockerroom," Mendez said. "We had a team meeting without the coaches (to try to ease the tension). It was a real sick feeling, because you felt tense and you didn't even want to go to practice."

Seeing his reclamation project crumbling at the foundation before the final shingles were put on the roof, Snyder called a meeting of team captains in his office. "The leaders surfaced and began to hold each other more accountable for their practice habits, for their lockerroom demeanor, and their attitudes," Snyder said. "I think that was what was needed. We had to have that before any real positive things could take place."

Mendez says the meeting helped. "Coach Snyder had a meeting with the captains alone and he said, 'You guys lead this team, juniors included,' which meant Quentin and me. So we had another team meeting, and I got up and told everyone, 'I don't give a (hoot) who you are; we're a team. We win together and we lose together.'"

It worked.

The week after the Colorado game, the Wildcats completed a four-game road stretch with a trip to Norman, Oklahoma, and a match-up against the Oklahoma Sooners. The Sooners owned a 21-game winning streak against Kansas State, with the average score in those games being 44-12. But Kansas State did not dwell on the previous three weeks heading into the game, much less the previous 21 years.

"At this particular time we had to go back and really do the best job we could of being able to assess our football team, and assess what we were capable of doing and what we were not capable of doing," Snyder said. "Then we had to work on those things that we were capable of doing and circumvent or eliminate all those things that we just at one time may have thought we were capable of doing, but weren't capable of doing. We put a great deal of emphasis on one of our team goals and that was not beating ourselves. It's easy to split up under these kinds of circumstances. Kansas State history for 100 years was to do exactly that. So that was that. Sometimes before you can unify, you have to have a little adversity.

"We began a lot more contact work. There are several philosophies, and one of them is when it really gets tough like that, then you really lighten the load, and you get everybody back in a better frame of mind. That's just not our approach. That had been the approach before, and consequently, in this fragile program, it did not work. Our approach was to get tougher. We were going to get ourselves out of the hole, because we were capable of it. The players were capable of it. We needed to be tough enough to deal with it and work through our problems.

The Cats' stepped-up efforts paid off early, as they took the lead on a 1-yard quarterback sneak in the first quarter, but OU answered with a Scott Blanton field goal and a Steve Collins-to-Albert Hall 4-yard TD pass to take a 10-7 lead. In the second quarter, another quarterback sneak gave the Cats a 14-10 lead. Two more Blanton field goals made it 16-14 at halftime.

In the third, the Cats moved to the OU 11-yard line, where they had first-and-10. They only gained 1 yard on three plays, so Snyder sent in Warren Claassen to try a 27-yard field goal. Claassen thought he hit it just inside the right upright, but the official ruled it wide, and the Sooners held on to the lead. "It went over the top of the right upright, and that makes it the official's judgment," Claassen said. "It was just on the inside of the upright, I think."

With Claassen's attempt ruled no good, neither team scored in the second half, as Kansas State's defense held the Sooners to just 83 yards in the half. The Cats, who had totaled 271 yards in the previous three games *combined*, gained 224 for the game.

"At the conclusion of that ballgame, as disappointed as everybody was, we realized that we had stopped the spiral, and we were in a position to begin the steps to get bet-

Snyder called a meeting of the team captains to help lead the team out of the doldrums. The 1992 captains were (from left): Matt Garber, Chris Patterson, Reggie Blackwell, Quentin Neujahr, Eric Gallon, Jaime Mendez and Brooks Barta.

ter and do what we should have done at the very beginning of the season," Snyder said.

The Wildcats finally returned home for a game against Iowa State, but more than the friendly faces around KSU stadium awaited. ESPN had selected the game as its Thursday night Game of the Week heading into the season, meaning the Cats would play on national television for the first time in 10 years.

The Wildcats were confronted with two options. Fresh off a four-game losing streak, the Cats could rebound and defeat a team against which it matched up favorably, thereby showing the country that Kansas State had arrived. Or they could continue their miserable ways and deal a severe blow to the respect the program had gained, locally, in the conference and nationally.

Snyder did not feel the pressure, especially from a national standpoint. "Kansas State wasn't a household word at that particular time," he said. "I don't know how many people across the country were very much aware of what had taken place during the course of our season, so an awful lot of people were seeing Kansas State for the first time. This could have been an upper division team of the Big 8, or the lower division, they didn't know. They were just seeing a ballgame for the most part. Consequently it came off very favorably."

The Cats were acquitted with an exceptional effort by the special teams and the defense. Kitt Rawlings and Thomas Randolph each blocked punts in the first quarter, setting up short touchdown drives that gave KSU a 12-0 halftime lead. The defense also turned in a big effort with three Masters interceptions and double figures in tackles for all three linebackers. Venables led with 21 takedowns.

"That game was going to put Kansas State on the map," Venables said. "We showed people that we're not as bad as you might have thought we were. Wow, it was great.

"It was a real smooth, comfortable game, almost a relaxing game. The defensive effort was really good. What really was gratifying about it was that we hadn't played that kind of team (a triple-option offense) all year, so it takes a lot of preparation on a short week. I know (linebackers coach Jim) Leavitt was real proud. His linebackers had more than 50 tackles."

With the short field the blocked punts and Masters' interceptions provided and a steady running game, the offense played one of its better games of the season. The passing game was left on the sideline. In the last two games, the Cats had completed a total of 10 passes (attempting only 20) for 104 yards. But the Cats gained 201 yards on the ground, including 164 by Gallon.

"We're trying to circumvent our weaknesses and play to whatever strengths we have, and do so trying not to beat ourselves," Snyder said.

Gallon moved into second place on the all-time career yardage chart with 1,874 yards. With three games left in his career, he was 309 yards behind Isaac Jackson for the all-time mark.

But Gallon was happier to be on the positive side of the scoreboard. The yardage marks were secondary. "I was telling the guys over and over again, it doesn't matter whether I get the yards or not as long as we get the W," Gallon said, looking back.

The Wildcats had improved to 4-4 and still had an opportunity for a winning season. It wasn't the type of improvement K-Staters had been looking for, but after the longest losing streak in four seasons, it was comforting to get back on the correct side of the ledger. And the victory had showed those K-Staters that a team coached by Bill Snyder would not give up. It was not just a slogan – Goal No. 8 on The Wildcat's Fourteen

Goals for Success – it was an attitude. A way of life.

Holthus, who had announced Kansas State games since 1984, talks about how the team's response to 1992 shows just how far the Cats had come under Snyder. "It was a benchmark year for the program," he said. "In the past, if Kansas State would have gone through the three horrible weeks of Kansas, Utah State and Colorado, it would have taken them five years to recover. For Coach Snyder, it took five days. They were just a controversial field goal away from winning at Oklahoma. Prior to Coach, this team would have finished 3-8, probably 2-9 the next year. So the fact that they slipped six inches rather than six feet was telling the people who were close to the program that something was different.

"They figured out a way to win at Iowa State. That's a cliche but they blocked two punts. They saw that Iowa State was vulnerable in their punt team and they were going after them. We didn't return punts that year. We lined up 10 guys on the line of scrimmage and said, 'Go for it.' So it was Coach saying, 'I'm going to find a way to win. If I've got to block punts, and have my son kick 55-yard punts, that's the way we're going to win. It was like bunting the runner home and winning 1-0."

Sean Snyder did punt the ball a long way in 1992. He earned consensus all-America status, the first K-Stater to achieve that honor since Gary Spani in 1977. "Coach deserved that," Holthus said. "That was a little reward for him. He hasn't had a lot of rewards. Maybe he's been given good financial compensation and he's been Coach of the Year and all that, but he took the risk of his career to come here, and he deserves whatever he wants. For him to see Sean become an all-American and be a part of this

---

Eric Gallon's whole world came crashing down April 4, 1992.

He was coming off a season in which he had gained 1,102 yards, the second-highest total in Kansas State history. He needed only 928 yards to break the all-time school record for yards in a career. A second-team all-Big Eight selection his junior year, he had all-America aspirations for the upcoming season. Then, during the first scrimmage of spring practice, he planted his right foot and heard a pop in his knee.

Coach Bill Snyder was upset when he first got to Gallon because Gallon was wearing the wrong shoes. "We have different shoes depending on the weather conditions, for safety purposes," he said. "Everybody wants to be at their best when they scrimmage, and Eric slipped by someone's scrutiny. Whether those shoes actually caused the injury or not, I wouldn't speculate."

Nobody realized at the time how serious the injury was. Gallon, in fact, wanted to get back in the scrimmage in a couple of plays. As a precaution, the trainer put Gallon on the cart and took him into the lockerroom, where he was examined by the team doctor. Dr. Bill Jones determined that Gallon's anterior cruciate ligament was torn, which meant that Gallon not only was through for the day and the rest of the spring, but his status for his senior season was in serious jeopardy.

"From that point, I grew upset," Gallon said. "I started crying. I was boo-hooing crying. I can't say it was just tears, I was boo-hooing. I just wanted to get away from everybody. I was able to walk from the training room. I walked back to the lockerroom, got undressed, and went to take a shower. As I tried to step down from a step, my knee went sliding to the right. The bottom part of my leg was to the left. I could still walk on it, but I knew that something was really wrong."

Gallon was despondent. He got dressed, threw his stuff into his bag and headed toward the parking lot and his truck. He was going to head back to his dorm, from where he would head home to Florida. "I was going to give up school and everything," Gallon said.

Word got out to the field, where Snyder still was conducting the scrimmage. He left the field and met Gallon at his truck, just before he got away. "It was an emotional scene," Snyder said. "He and I were both in tears. I felt so badly because there was that threat that he would never play again. He knew the ramifications of what this kind of knee injury could do to his career.

"I promised him that he would play this game again. He would have to work hard. He would have to have a great deal of courage, but everybody would support him. We would do everything in our power to help him. And if he would help himself, he could come back and would be able to play again. I told him that I couldn't promise him that it would be here, but he would come back and have the opportunity to play again."

Gallon found it hard to believe he could play again, but he knew he could believe Snyder. "I talked with our trainer and he told me about a new procedure

remarkable story, is a little something extra that people may have taken for granted. To have it happen for his family made it really neat."

Always the coach, Snyder gives the credit for the adjustments back to the players and his coaches. "We were just trying to avoid beating ourselves and do the things we could do best," Snyder said. "We tried to put greater emphasis on those things and give them a chance to excel. We had great preparation in our specialty teams and consequently won the game with them. We thought we could block some punts and we did and that set the tone for the ballgame."

"I really believe the first game of the 1993 season was the Iowa State game in 1992," Thomas Randolph said. "We were at home. It was our last home game and it was on ESPN. We're not the greatest team, but we're going to show the country that we can play football at Kansas State. We were going to do it through special teams, offense and defense. All of us were going to try to win the game. We all came through."

that would allow me to play again in six to eight months. That would put me back by mid-season." That was looking at the optimistic six-month prognosis.

"I went back to my dorm and prayed about it with my roommate, T. Price," he said. "I prayed that I could be back before the season started. Then I told T., 'I am not going to say anything else about it. I'm going to leave it in God's hands.'"

Gallon then put wheels under his prayers. After a successful surgery by Dr. Jones, Gallon went to work. "I was going in in the mornings, maybe 7:00, 7:30, 8:00. I wouldn't leave until lunch time and then I would come back in the afternoon about 3:00. I wouldn't leave until about 7:00. I was spending a lot of time trying to rehab every day. This was on Saturdays and Sundays, too. That was my weekend. I couldn't go out or anything. I couldn't be on the knee, couldn't stand up. I was restricted to my room and the training room."

Gallon also got a little unusual help in his rehab. "Coach Snyder did every-

thing when I was in the hospital," Gallon said. "He knew my favorite hamburger was a Quarterpounder. He brought one to me every night."

Snyder wanted to do everything he could to make the recovery go smoother. He knew that the mental part of Gallon's comeback would be just as tough as the physical part. "Eric worked extremely hard," Snyder said. "He had long, hard, painful work. He had to overcome the mental aspect of it on several occasions when it was just too much, it was not worth it. He had several opportunities to say, 'Let's forget this, let's go home and heal like a normal person heals.' But he didn't. He stayed and worked hard."

All that work paid off earlier than anyone, except Gallon and Snyder, had figured possible. On the second offensive play in the first game of the season, J.J. Smith turned his ankle. Gallon jogged onto the field greeted by a stand-

ing ovation. He gained 87 yards on 22 carries. The next week, he gained 134 yards and was named the Big Eight Offensive Player of the Week. Gallon was back.

He finished his career as the second-leading rusher in school history. He then signed as a free agent with the New England Patriots. He injured his hamstring and didn't get to play in the NFL, though he still harbors the thought of trying again.

He now looks on those values that helped him make a miraculous recovery as a base for the rest of his life. "One of Coach's 14 goals is 'Never Give Up,'" he said. "That's what made me want to go out every day and put forth the effort I did in the training room. There were a lot of times that they would tell me that a lot of kids would give up at that point. But I didn't. I didn't want to be in that category."

The Wildcats lost 27-14 to Missouri the following week, temporarily stumbling back into their pattern from the midseason. The Cats trailed 10-7 late in the first half when they fumbled a punt. The Tigers capitalized with a touchdown to increase the halftime lead to 17-7. Ten more points in the third quarter gave the Tigers a 27-7 lead that the Cats could not overcome.

"It was just a game that we didn't show up for at all," Venables said.

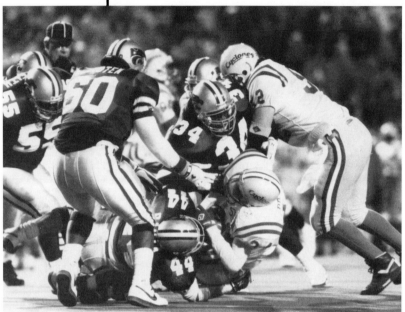

The loss left the Cats with the prospect of having to defeat Oklahoma State and Nebraska to earn a winning record. The Cowboys came to Manhattan with a 4-5-1 record and a chance at their first .500 season since they went 10-2 in 1988 with Heisman Trophy winner Barry Sanders.

The offense did what it had to do and the defense dominated for Kansas State, shutting out the Cowboys in a 10-0 victory. The defense recovered two fumbles, blocked a field goal and picked off four OSU passes, giving the Cats 21 for the season, which set a school record. Of the four, Masters and Mendez each had one. Masters' was the seventh of 1992, a school record, and Mendez placed himself on the all-time

Defense and special teams carried the Cats in 1992, never moreso than against Iowa State, stopping KSU's four-game losing streak.

charts with the 13th of his career.

"It was gratifying to do it for the seniors, to send them away from Kansas State as winners," Mendez said. "Defensively we knew we had to win the football game. So it just showed that we had the determination, we were going to fight even though we were playing with one gun. We knew we had to find a way to win and we did."

The offense managed only 198 yards of total offense, but eight of them came on a scoring run by Toby Lawrence – offensive lineman Toby Lawrence. With the score 3-0 at the start of the second quarter, the Cats had the ball at the OSU 8. Lawrence picked up the ball on the *fumblerooski* play and rumbled into the end zone for the first score of his career.

"I probably waddled more into the end zone," Lawrence said. "I was just trying to be as cool as possible and was hoping we wouldn't get a penalty or anything."

The victory assured the Cats of its first undefeated home season in 58 years. It gave the seniors a victory in their last home game and extended the Wildcats' home record to 15-2 in the past three seasons. And it left alive the hopes for a winning campaign.

The Cats traveled to Tokyo, Japan, for their final contest of the year, the Coca-Cola Bowl against Nebraska. The game itself quickly became an afterthought.

"There was no doubt that we were playing second fiddle in this band," Neujahr said. "The whole Coca Cola Bowl was centered around getting Nebraska in Tokyo. They could care less if it were Kansas State or anybody else. It could be Surprise Tech for all they cared."

Snyder had made certain requests when the contract was signed. He wanted to be sure the Wildcats would be treated equally and would not agree to the game until he was given assurances. Unfortunately, some of those assurances didn't amount to anything.

Snyder grew testy when his team arrived at a banquet to find out that the meal would not start for another hour and a half, because Nebraska had been delayed from their practice. Not only could the Cats not eat dinner, they were not allowed to enter the ballroom to snack on the hors d'oeuvres. "They provide a dinner to which both teams are invited, along with a lot of dignitaries and some entertainment," Snyder said. "I always am concerned about promptness and time. I don't want our players to be anywhere a half-hour early or a half-hour late. We have what we call 'Cat-time.' That's being five minutes early. Wherever we go, we're five minutes early. That allows us all to conserve time, and it's not a dollar waiting on a dime. We want to show respect for any function with which we happen to be involved.

"I had checked on countless occasions to be sure about exactly what time we were expected to be at the dinner. We were expected to be there at 5:00, so that's when we showed up. It wasn't that they weren't ready, it was that Nebraska was not there. They

Thomas Randolph recorded one of the two blocked punts against Iowa State that was 'the first game of the 1993 season.'

wanted to hold up everything until Nebraska got there. I didn't mean to go on with the program. Our players very simply could have gone in and had hors d'oeuvres and some soda. They were hungry. Their dinner had been delayed an hour waiting for Nebraska.

"I couldn't find the fellow who was in charge of the whole thing, so I found a young lady who was assisting him. I told her that I wanted them to open the doors and allow our players in. She resisted that, and I said, 'You have two options: you open the doors now, or we will not be here for the event, period.' That was it. I was prepared to take our team back to the hotel. So she opened the doors and let the players in. It hurt nothing and I certainly was not rude to the young lady."

But the treatment at the banquet was symptomatic of the way the Wildcats were treated during most of the trip. "The very first thing that happened was when the poster came out," Snyder said. "The poster was to be distributed to advertise the ballgame itself. The company that promoted all this sent it out and wanted us to distribute it with our boosters to help sell tickets. Every player on the poster was in a red uniform. Coca Cola is red, I understand that, but that's a lack of sensitivity toward our players. I threw them all away.

"I wanted just one thing. I wanted our football team to be treated with respect. I wanted our players to be respected by the people who put on the bowl game. This was a neutral sight. They had recruited both teams. I didn't want our players to feel less

Brooks Barta's leadership helped the Cats right the ship in 1992.

wanted, to feel that they were there on a coattail. I just wanted them to be paid due respect. Nebraska was willing to do that. We never had a problem with the University of Nebraska or (head coach) Tom (Osborne). Those are all quality people, and it was a very pleasant experience. But that wasn't the case with the people who handled the organization of the ballgame itself."

The players appreciated Snyder's persistence. "All the things that they did nice for us, Coach Snyder requested," Neujahr said. "A lot of the things that Coach Snyder stuck up for us, they still bypassed. They said, 'We've got you here now, what are you going to do, pack up your bags and go home? It's going to cost your school a lot of money and a lot of embarrassment. You won't do that.' Having Coach Snyder definitely helped us. We really would have gotten the shaft if Coach Snyder weren't on our side.

"We'd still be in downtown Tokyo somewhere."

At least the field itself seemed safe. Not quite. After being told he could choose the side of the field his team would occupy, Snyder was told to take his team to the other side right before game time. "I had talked with them on countless occasions about which side of the field we were going to be on," he said. "They had told me which side we would be on, which wasn't the side we ended up on. I didn't want to be on the same side

the band was going to be on. I didn't want the band blaring in our players' ears.

"Obviously the best thing would have been for them to move the band, and then it wouldn't have been a problem. But we were told that we would be on that side, and when we came out for the pregame warmup, the benches had been switched. Our people were told to put their stuff on the other side of the field. I had three options. One was to argue about it, one was to accept it, and the third one was to go in the lockerroom and stay there. I didn't want to do that. You're talking about a television audience and a lot of people who came, and I didn't want a lot of people to suffer for the errors of two or three people. At that time I didn't want to carry this battle on with our players. I didn't want them to be disrupted in terms of their focus, so I accepted it."

Once the game got rolling, the Wildcats gave the Huskers a run for their money. Nebraska jumped out to a 21-0 lead in the second quarter before senior Matt Garber led the Cats on two scoring drives. He hit Andre Coleman with a 10-yard strike to finish the first drive and Tate Wright booted a 40-yard field goal to close the first half scoring.

Nebraska answered with 10 points to start the third quarter to pull away safely. Garber scored on an 8-yard run and threw a 21-yard pass to Brad Seib to make the final score respectable. Garber's 246 yards was a career high, as were the 19 completions on 29 attempts. "It's nice to go out on a bang," he said, "not a big enough bang, but a little one."

"I was as proud of Matt's performance as any we've had since we've been here," Snyder said.

It was the first visit to a domed stadium for any of the current Wildcats. That, too, was something they wouldn't soon forget. "I remember walking into that dome thinking, 'This is going to be cool, nice and breezy, relaxed, a great atmosphere to play a game,"

The mixture of Japanese and American signage made for an interesting backdrop.

Neujahr recalled. "It was hotter than donut grease in there. I remember coming off the field after warmups being ringing wet. It was incredible, the amount of humidity that was in the dome. I also remember walking on the turf and thinking, 'We had better turf back at Kansas State in 1990 than this stuff.'

"I remember the crowd being secluded from the game, not really on top of you. They knew when to cheer, specific moments. But they really didn't know what football is all about, what a fourth-and-one is, what a third-and-10 is. They knew the basics. They knew a touchdown, they

It finally happened. A man named Snyder came to Manhattan, Kansas, and through sheer determination and hard work, he helped turn the Kansas State football program into a winner. Individually, he received national recognition as the best at his job in the country.

Boy, was his *dad* proud.

Sean Snyder came to Kansas State, where he rejoined his father, head coach Bill Snyder, in 1990 after two years at the University of Iowa. After a redshirt year, he punted for the Wildcats in 1991 and 1992. Following the 1992 season, he was named a consensus all-America, just the second player so-honored in the school's history.

Actually, there are more similarities between father and son than on-field success. They both always have wanted what's best for the other, even though often it meant separation. Sean was just finishing his redshirt season at Iowa when Bill was approached about the job at Kansas State. As talks grew more serious, Bill talked to numerous colleagues and friends about whether it was a wise decision. Most people said it was an opportunity that he should take. But there was one vote of approval he needed above all.

"Sean was the last person whom I addressed with the issue, because he was with me at Iowa," Bill said. "I wouldn't have come if he didn't share his blessing. He wanted me to make that move, so I felt more comfortable doing it. He came to the University of Iowa because I was there and I loved him far too much to leave him if he weren't comfortable with it."

While Sean did not know his vote could outweigh all the others, he did know that his opinion would be influential. "If I had told him that I didn't really care for him to go, I don't think he would have," he said. "The fact of me wanting to be with him, and him wanting to be with me, was real strong. But I've always wanted the best for him, and he's always wanted the best for me, too."

Sean switched the roles in his mind, which confirmed his decision.

"I've always wanted to play in the NFL," he said. "I didn't go to college to transfer, but I wasn't going to go to a college and sit on the bench if I thought I could play. I've always thought I could play the game, so I left. I would have done the same thing if he were still coaching there. If it came down to where I was sitting on the bench, and I thought I could have been playing, I don't think I could have sat there and watched someone else do it, even if he were still at Iowa. I'm sure that he would have approved of that if it would lead into something better.

"Stepping in front of him being a head coach would bother me. I did want to be in the same place as he was, and if the (KSU coaching) opportunity hadn't come up, then that would have been wonderful. I would have enjoyed it just as much if he didn't go there. But the fact that he did, I was happy for him."

Sean also was not surprised that the offer was there. It was just a matter of time before his father got his chance.

"I knew that this was the opportunity that he had been looking for, the chance to take over a program, to rehabilitate it, to take it wherever he could go with it," he said. "And he's worked hard at it. I think he's the most deserving person in the world to have that happen, to get a head coaching job and do that. He's paid his dues.

"The conversation lasted five min-

knew a field goal, they knew extra point. The atmosphere just wasn't there."

Following the game, both teams were supposed to remain on the field for the trophy and player-of-the-game presentations. At least that's what Snyder was told before the game. But when the final gun sounded, Snyder was asked to bring Coleman, K-State's MVP, to the center of the field and send the rest of his team into the lockerroom. It was the final straw.

"I told them, 'Our football team was told that they would be out here. If you can't have my football team, you can't have me,'" Snyder said. "It was my assumption that Andre was a part of our football team and that he would have understood it. I didn't think he would have chosen to send his teammates in while he accepted the award."

"I was very disappointed, but I didn't know Coach Snyder's reasoning when it hap-

utes. I mean it was quick. I didn't have a second thought. It was, 'I want you to take that, because it's been what you've been waiting for. Why coach if you can't make it to the top.' You won't find a coach in the world who is happy being an assistant. Everybody wants to be a head coach."

Sean and Bill have specialized in five-minute conversations. After Sean came to Kansas State, one of the highlights for his dad was the daily, private visits after practice. "I had an opportunity to be around him and spend time with him," Bill said. "We managed to spend time, not so much on the field, but off the field. It wasn't extensive, but we got in our 10 minutes a day, every day, and that was important to me.

"I've always been hard on Sean, as I have with all our children, but they mean absolutely everything to me. It was enjoyable to be able to (spend time with Sean)."

Those times are what made the three years together in Manhattan special. "Yes, it was wonderful," Sean said. "I think of everything that's happened in my college career, the best thing was playing for him. There's not many people who get that chance. There's a lot of coaches and a lot of coaches' sons who play. But most don't step into a program that hasn't won a game in three years and get a chance to play on a team that actually makes national headline news, not to mention have your dad as head coach."

As Ozzie-and-Harriet as that might sound, it's not the only reason the younger Snyder chose to transfer to Kansas State. He was recruited to Iowa as a punter and a place kicker. After sitting out his freshman year, he was tabbed to be the starting punter in the fall of 1989. He punted one game, and was benched. Although he liked Iowa City and the program at Iowa, he looked to move to a place where he could play.

Kansas State fit the bill.

The Wildcats' punter, Chris Cobb, had one year left, which meant that after Sean sat out the required one year after transferring, the starting job would be open for competition. Sean was confident he could win the job. "They were graduating their punter and a kicker, so all the jobs were coming open," he said. "Not only was my dad there, but the jobs were open for someone to take. I went right in and competed for the job. It was the opportunity for me to play, moreso than a lot of other places where I'd have to go in and compete against whomever was the starter."

Sean was not the automatic starter, however. Matt Argo, a walk-on, and the younger Snyder battled through training camp to see who would earn the scholarship as the starting punter. "Sean came as a walk-on and had to earn a scholarship, and that's the way he wanted it," Bill Snyder said. "Matt was the heir apparent. They competed for the position very closely. We went with Sean because he was the underclassman. That's our policy when there are two players who battle equally, because the underclassman has a chance to contribute to the program longer."

Sean worked hard, another trait he shares with his father. The work paid off, as he was tabbed first-team all-America by the Associated Press, the Kodak Coaches Poll and Athlons, some of the same organizations that honored his father with their coaching awards.

Sean believes his father will stay at Kansas State as long as there is a challenge. "I think my dad has a drive to always want a challenge," he said. "There's still a challenge there. Everybody has heard of Kansas State now, but they want to see how good they really are, because nobody really knows. They'll say, 'OK, they got lucky. They went 9-2-1. They tied Colorado, they're getting close to Nebraska and they beat Oklahoma. Whoopee.' No one has as much faith in the program as the players and coaches. There's no doubt if you ask a player, 'Are you guys going to win next year?,' they'll say, 'Yes, we are.' If you had asked them that five years ago, they would have said, 'I don't know.'

"The expectations are high, now. It's not fair that when a program finally achieves success that people will grumble if the level falls off. But I don't think anybody in the world would play sports if it were written how it was going to finish. It's the challenge of making history, so to say. It would be like writing a book. Nobody wants to read a book if you know the end of it. There's no sense in reading it, if you know what's going to happen."

pened," Coleman said. "After he explained it to me, I was perfectly fine. Kansas State had been fighting for respect for a long time. They didn't give us respect and treat us very fairly over there. I don't blame Coach Snyder for doing exactly what he did."

Snyder, Coleman and the rest of the Cats all headed for the lockerroom and quickly to the team hotel. Snyder had KSU sports information director Ben Boyle tell the media that he and the players would be available to talk to anyone at the hotel.

It still bothers Snyder that he received criticism back home for his complaints in Tokyo. "I'm old enough and hard enough to deal with that," he said. "What angered me was that these were people writing about these things when they were 15 hours away from the scene. These were all people who weren't in Tokyo. They weren't with our team. We didn't have any (local beat writers) there, but they've all got a lot to say about it. They were inaccurate. They had half the story."

The lack of respect, and the fact that Kansas State had fallen short against the Cornhuskers, made for a disappointing finish to 1992. But it also set the stage for the biggest step yet.

At least the field of play seems like home to the Cats, who made a respectable showing against Nebraska.

Coleman (opposite page) had an outstanding game at the Coca-Cola Bowl, just a prelude to an all-America year in 1993.

1993
THE PROMISED LAND

Old habits die hard. For years, when the Big Eight Skywriters got together to make their preseason picks, Kansas State was the automatic choice for eighth place. Even coming off a 5-6 1990 season, the Cats were tabbed for last in 1991. Finally, a 7-4 record brought the pundits to their senses and they predicted the Cats would escape the cellar and finish fifth in 1992.

They did, but they didn't. A disappointing 2-5 record in the conference left the Wildcats tied for sixth (and last).

So when the Skywriters made their predictions for 1993, guess where Kansas State was listed. Yep, eighth.

"They've been doing it for so long," Snyder said at the beginning of the '93 season, "we are written in that position before the ballots are handed out."

The Skywriters were dead wrong this time. This team was ready to make amends for 1992. "It was a learning experience," senior receiver Andre Coleman said. "We learned that success is not going to be handed to us. Guys took things for granted.

"Everyone vowed that will never happen again. And the only way to keep that from happening is to work hard. I know we say the attitude is better every year, but it's been 105 degrees outside and guys want to go out to practice. We're hungry."

That hunger paid off, as the Cats gobbled up arguably the best season in school history.

If the Kansas State Wildcats took "baby steps" of progress in Bill Snyder's first season, and "crossed the line" in his third year in Manhattan, 1993 was a trip to The Promised Land. Once again, the Wildcats were "two feet from the Orange Bowl," but this time the inches didn't keep them from the post-season celebrating. The season culminated in the school's second-ever bowl berth, a 52-17 victory over Wyoming in the Weiser Lock Copper Bowl.

The team's nine wins was the most in 83 years and a 1-1-1 record versus the conference's "Big Three" (Nebraska, Colorado and Oklahoma) led to a third-place Big Eight finish. Riding the conference's best non-league mark (14-3, including bowl games) since 1990 and a school-best 13-game home unbeaten streak, the Cats finished the season in the Top 20 for the first time. Ever.

End zone celebrations covered with purple were commonplace with the Wildcats' offensive firepower in 1993.

Some may call the Wildcats' rise to national prominence a Cinderella story. But the real story is no fairy tale, and was not merely a wish granted. The Wildcats earned their success.

There were the required blowouts that a Top-20 team must have. There were the close games, too. The Cats played other nationally ranked teams well and even threw in the remarkable come-from-behind, against-all-odds win that solidifies a team as a bonafide contender.

"It certainly was a very established goal with our players," Snyder said of the goal of appearing in a bowl game. "The preseason talk among our players was very much focused on the opportunity to go to a bowl. Here were a lot of seniors who had been here through the whole turnaround. They were here from the beginning.

President Jon Wefald unveiled the sign proclaiming the new Dev Nelson Press Box for Mrs. Nelson and the rest of the crowd at the dedication ceremony.

"This wasn't a breakthrough year. We won more ballgames than we did in other years, but if you had a breakthrough year, maybe you would have to identify it as '91. I think each one is just a step, it's just a progression that takes place. What I always relate to is the foundation that was established in '89, and bricks continually were being laid on the foundation. So things that happened in 1989 had a very direct impact on the outcome of the '93 season."

The strength of the team was reflected in the post-season honors that the team earned. Snyder earned national coach of the year consideration for the second time in three seasons and three of his players (Coleman, Jaime Mendez and Thomas Randolph) earned Associated Press All-America status. Mendez was the Cats' second consensus all-America in as many years (punter Sean Snyder in 1992).

Two more additions to the sports complex also hinted at the program's entrenchment as one of the conference's best equipped. The Dev Nelson Press Box, a $3.3 million five-level facility rises above the stadium on the west side, and a $2.2 million indoor practice facility enables the Cats to practice all aspects of their game simultaneously. It is a 130-yard facility with a roof high enough to practice all kicking drills, as well.

While Snyder acknowledges that facilities alone do not make the program, he is grateful to those who were instrumental in enhancing that segment of the program. These improvements bring the total dollar figure to more than $8 million since Snyder took over in 1989. "Obviously, I always will be grateful to those who believed strongly enough in the entirety of our program to fund such an endeavor," Snyder said. "It's a piece of the whole scenario. Everything has its place.

"Yes, it does have an impact on everything. The young people in our program and the coaching staff need to see that there is progress being made. There always is evidence that there is something coming."

As nice as the complex was, it did not make up for a disappointing 1992. "We were saying the same thing at the conclusion of the '92 season, that we were saying beginning our preparation for '93," Snyder said. "It was the same thing we said at the end of the '91 season, going into 1992. 'Yes, we've done something, but don't take this for granted.' Leading into 1993, we were saying, 'OK, this is what happens when you take something for granted.' We had a number of quality players back and we had experience. There were a lot of positive things going into the '93 season."

A winable non-conference schedule began with home games against New Mexico State and Western Kentucky. The Cats were lackadaisical in the first half of both games, holding halftime leads of 10-7 and 14-13, respectively. But the offense kicked in in the second half, scoring 24 points in each game to register 24- and 25-point wins.

"We weren't quite as sharp as we needed to be and yet at the same time, it was early in the season, and our goal, as always, was to try to get a little bit better all the time," Snyder said. "You've got to see where you are and try to build on it as you go. We had a quarterback who never had played in our system and had only had the benefit of spring football. He was making that

Nothing seemed out of reach for Coleman and the Cats in 1993.

131

improvement on a very regular basis and that was part of our team getting a little bit better as we progressed through the season."

The Cats entered the third game of the season at

It's the stuff of legend. One day during fall drills in 1993, Andre Coleman was quizzing quarterback Chad May on the strength of his arm. Just how far could May throw it, Coleman wanted to know.

May stood on the 20-yard line and sent Coleman deep. Real deep. And then he overthrew him. When the ball fell back to Earth, it landed *out of the other end zone.*

"Chad's kind of a cocky kid, which is what I think we needed at the quarterback position," Coleman said. "I would tease him and tell him there were other quarterbacks around the nation who had stronger arms. One day, I was teasing him about a quarterback, and I said, 'That quarterback, he can throw it 75 yards.' Chad said, 'I can throw it 80.' I said, 'Yeah, right.' Then I went down to the end zone and he stood on the 20, and he threw it out of the end zone.

"I just walked off the field. I didn't say anything to him."

May did a lot of throwing, long and short, in 1993. He set three Big Eight records and added four other Kansas State records. Against Nebraska, May completed a KSU-record 30 passes for 489 yards. It was the highest total ever in a Big Eight game. In many opinions, he was the best quarterback in a quarterback-laden conference.

"There are some excellent quarterbacks in this league, but Chad went head-to-head with Tommie Frazier, Kordell Stewart and Cale Gundy and didn't come out on the short end of the stick against anyone," Bill Snyder said. "He's my all-Big Eight quarterback."

May's day against the Cornhuskers helped him throw for 2,682 yards for the season, surpassing easily Lynn Dickey's KSU mark of 2,476 yards. It was the third highest total in conference history, the second highest in an 11-game season and the highest ever by a junior QB. He gained those yards on just 350 attempts, which established a conference mark for the highest average yards per attempt (7.64). He also set a conference mark for consecutive games with a TD pass with 10. He also set school marks for touchdowns in a season and

2-0 for the fourth straight year. But with all the success experienced by Kansas State under Snyder, there still remained one atrocious streak. The Wildcats had not won a non-conference game on the road since 1979, a string of 16 games. They traveled to Minneapolis for a game against the University of Minnesota with a chance to exorcise the last demon from past regimes.

It was one of those wins that a Top-20 team is supposed to get. The Wildcats zoomed to a 17-0 lead in the first half and then put it into cruise. Unfortunately, the auto pilot malfunctioned and the Gophers got right back into the game. Chad May's first interception of the year bounced off a defender and into the arms of Jeff Rosga, who ran it back 25 yards for the score. Then, with 4:14 left in the first half, Tim Schade threw 18 yards to Chuck Rios and the Cats' lead was 17-13 at halftime.

Neither team scored in the third and K-State got the first score of the fourth quarter when May ran in from the 7. But then the wheels fell off. Schade hit Aaron Osterman for a 9-yard TD. The try for two was no good and the Cats led, 24-19. With

total offense.

It's a good thing that May's numbers speak loudly about his talent. That's about the only way you'll get him to say much. When asked why he chose Kansas State after deciding to leave Cal-State Fullerton, he said, "They threw the ball and I liked the offense they were running." Pretty much to the point, which is how May handles most things.

May was an outstanding high school baseball player who didn't play football until his senior year. He was recruited by such baseball powers as Arizona State and Pepperdine, but he chose Fullerton, because they allowed him to play football.

"All these schools wanted me to play baseball," he said. "People like to look at you during your junior season, and I hadn't played football. That kind of hurt me. But I had a love for football. My dad always told me I was better at baseball, but I just wanted to throw the football, so that's what I chose."

During his year of action at Fullerton, he had second thoughts about his decision. It certainly was easier to handle a hot grounder at third than it was to be a punching bag to 275-pound linemen who constantly were in his face.

"Everyone would watch films and just bring the house," he said of the opponents at Fullerton. "They would rush eight people. Sometimes, people were beating me back on my drop and sacking me. It was not fun.

"I was always in getting treatment. I kept getting hammered."

The constant pressure resulted in some ugly numbers. He threw only four touchdowns and nine interceptions. He completed only 42 percent of his passes (97 of 233) for 1,066 yards. "I was fed up during the year," he said. "I don't like to lose and we were getting blown out."

He considered leaving, but his decision was made much easier when he was called into head coach Gene Murphy's office the day after the last game. Murphy informed May that the Titans were switching to the option offense to better suit the team's roster. May, who is not quick, looked elsewhere. He took only one recruiting trip and decided that K-State would fit.

After watching Kansas State's offense struggle in 1992, he got his chance in '93. While the rest of the conference may have been shocked at his ability, the K-State coaching staff was not surprised at all. "I was pleased about it," Snyder said. "I wasn't surprised that he played well. He got better as the season went on. He was a very accomplished player when we finished."

"Chad's got an awfully strong arm," offensive coordinator Del Miller added. "He's a good competitor and he picked up our offensive schemes quickly."

May was selected first-team all-Big Eight by the coaches, and only honorable mention all-Big Eight by the media, a slight he passes off easily. "The coaches are the ones who have to prepare to stop me and know what I can do to a defense," he said. "I play against the coaches; I don't play against reporters. The coaches' poll is the one that counts in my mind."

May does not lack confidence. That was evident in the final regular season game at Oklahoma State. The Cats had fallen behind, 17-14, with 58 seconds left and had the ball at their own 20. May calmly drove them 80 yards in 41 seconds with no timeouts for the winning score.

"We just rolled," he said. "The defense softened up a little bit on us. It went so fast, I can't explain it. I knew we were going to score."

It's the attitude he takes with him every time he steps on the field. "I take each game the same," he said. "It doesn't matter if it's Kansas, Nebraska, Minnesota or Western Kentucky. I go out there to win every game and it doesn't matter who is standing in my way."

The offense exploded quickly against Minnesota, opening up a big early lead. May then directed the final scoring drive that reclaimed the lead in the fourth.

When Asheiki Preston (9) ran out of bounds on the final play (below), the Cats had claimed their second win in three years against KU and earned a 5-0 record.

5:33 remaining, May dropped back into his own end zone and was blindsided by Andy Kratochvil, jarring the ball loose. Craig Sauer recovered the ball and the Gophers led.

That's where the Cats' determination kicked in. Coleman ran back the ensuing kickoff 72 yards to the Minnesota 24. Four plays later, J.J. Smith scooted in from the 7 and the Cats led 30-25. But the Wildcats' efficiency hurt them because 3:11 still remained. Schade led the Gophers 76 yards to the KSU 4, where they had first-and-10 with 1:19 remaining. Three plays netted two yards.

Schade crouched under center with 52 seconds left, looking at fourth down. He fired the ball to Osterman, but the pass was just out of reach, and the Cats held. No longer was there a 14-year losing streak.

"That probably was as instrumental as any ballgame we played," Snyder said. "It really was a very dynamic ballgame and probably because so many different things took place. We learned so much from that ballgame.

"The game changed hands in so many different ways, so many different things had an impact on it. There was the defensive side of it, playing well at the very beginning, eventually allowing Minnesota to move the ball and then stopping the drive right on the brink of disaster at the very end. Offensively, we came out of the gate well, getting points on the board immediately, then turned over the ball twice, which allowed Minnesota to score 14 points, and then came back at the very

end when you had to have another touchdown. The kicking game and the specialty teams (contributed). It was a non-conference win on the road, which was one of those things that hadn't taken place since all of us were children. In the end, there was real emotion after that ballgame, probably as jubilant a lockerroom as I can recall here."

In each of the past three years, the Cats went through the non-conference season with a 3-1 record. They had not won all four non-conference games in a season since 1954. Make that 1993. After falling behind 14-10 at halftime to Nevada-Las Vegas, the Cats outscored the Rebels 26-6 in the second half to win, 36-20.

But that was small concern to the Wildcats. A perfect non-conference mark was not their goal for the season. A perfect season was.

"At that time I think everybody thought we were going to go 12-0 to be honest with you," senior center Quentin Neujahr said. "I don't think there was a soul who didn't think we were going to go up to Nebraska (the second Big Eight game) and win. I really don't think there was. I think everybody thought we were going to the Orange Bowl."

"You appreciate those kinds of thoughts, particularly coming from somebody whom you know is going to go back on the field and work every bit as hard today as he did yesterday," Snyder added. "Nothing is going to temper his work habits. Sometimes that kind of talk is loose cannon talk and you don't like to hear that. If you've got a young player who hasn't been around and hasn't gone through all these other things that these guys go through, then it's awful easy for them to talk in that vernacular. But Quentin had been here, and for him to say that and have that feeling, because he's a

With the wind blowing hard, the offenses had to rely on the ground game, something K-State enjoyed with J.J. Smith.

The crowd wasn't concerned about the margin; the win was all that mattered.

pretty realistic young guy, then I can appreciate that."

The real season began Saturday, October 9. The Kansas Jayhawks came to KSU Stadium for the Big Eight opener with all the excess baggage that goes along with a KU-K-State match-up. And, much like 1991, the Cats were on the verge of taking that next step. They had their sights set firmly on their first bowl berth in 11 years.

The Cats won the toss and elected to take the 25-mph wind at their backs. After holding KU on its first possession, the Cats marched 68 yards on their opening possession, culminated by May's 19-yard pass to Coleman. Later in the first, Tate Wright booted his career-best 50-yard field goal and

---

Late in the third quarter of Kansas State's 52-17 victory over Wyoming in the 1993 Copper Bowl, Mitch Holthus, the "Voice of the Wildcats," told the radio audience that Kevin Lockett, Kansas State's spectacular freshman receiver had been held without a catch. Almost as if he had his Walkman tuned to the Wildcat Network, Lockett sprinted down the left sideline and outleaped the Wyoming defender for a 30-yard reception and a 38-10 Cats lead.

It capped a season of great catches for Lockett, one in which he led the nation in yards (770), catches (50) and touchdowns (four) among freshman receivers. His 50 catches were a Big Eight-freshman record, and the 770 yards nearly doubled the previous high for yards by a freshman in the Big Eight. He also bettered the K-State mark for 100-yard receiving games with three. His 50 grabs were the seventh best and the 770 yards were the fourth best in team history.

And Lockett did it all with a big smile on his baby face. He looks more like a high-schooler than a big-time college receiver. "I've always been kidded about the baby face and the grin," he said. "I can't help but grin, especially after a good play or after our team does something well."

That creates quite a problem for defensive backs in Division I football who usually do a lot of trash-talking. When one player jaws at his opponent, the expectation is that the other player either will be rattled or will talk back. Not Lockett. "A lot of defenders like to talk trash to me," he said. "But I think when I make a good play and I turn around and smile, it just upsets them. When they talk a lot and then see me smile back, it really gets to them.

"Why I grin, I don't know. I try to have fun. I try not to take it so seriously, because I feel when I take it too seriously, it feels like a job, or it feels like I have some pressure to perform well. I just try to have fun and take everything in stride."

If Lockett's disposition doesn't get to the defense, his skills certainly do. He is not the fastest receiver on the field, and at 6-feet and 160 pounds, he's not the biggest, but big plays are his specialty. His 70 yards per game, which ranked second in the conference, speaks to that. "A lot of people say that I don't have the break-away speed that players like Andre Coleman had," he said. "But I think with me being so-called undersized, I've always had to try to find a way to progress, a way to move up and make

the plays."

Don't take his nonchalance as a lack of confidence. Head coach Bill Snyder describes him as "an achiever. He plays with great confidence. He just manages to get things done.

"He has a presence about him. There are people whom people are attracted to, and Kevin is one of them. He wasn't elected as a captain this year because he is so young, but he will function in the capacity of a leader. He already does have a leadership role because he does attract people to him."

As a senior at Tulsa's Washington High School, the same school that graduated Oklahoma basketball great Wayman Tisdale, he was recruited by Oklahoma State, Missouri and Southern Methodist, along with Kansas State. Oklahoma sent him "a couple of letters and made a couple of calls, but their recruiting coordinator and their wide receiver position coach felt that I was too small to play," he said. It came down to OSU and K-State, and he chose Kansas State because "it was like they were just one giant family," he said.

"(Coach Snyder) really cared about his players. Talking to a lot of the players on my recruiting trip, they really showed me that the players

the Cats held a 10-0 lead. Little did anyone know that KSU would not score again. That's not to say that the offense wasn't working.

Embarrassed by a minus-56-yard rushing effort and nine sacks allowed in the 1992 game, the offensive line set out to show that it could block. The result was a career-best, 135-yard rushing effort for J.J. Smith, 161 yards on the ground for the team and one sack allowed. "The way they beat us last year was a real embarrassment to us," tackle Jim Hmielewski said. "We were fired up for this. We felt like we had something to prove."

So, too, did the defense, which gave up 31 points in the previous year's game. Five KSU defenders tallied more than 10 tackles, led by Mendez' 19 and Kirby Hocutt's 16. Although they allowed the Jayhawks 354 yards of total offense, they never let them cross the goal line. And with KU holding the ball, and strong-legged Dan Eichloff pacing the sidelines, the Cats never let the Jayhawks get into field goal range for a last-second attempt, and left the fan-packed field with a 10-9 victory.

The Cats had a different reaction to the game than the fans did. While thousands

stuck together and he cared about his team."

Lockett made an impact early, catching his first touchdown in the season's second week, a 33-yarder against Western Kentucky. Against Nebraska, in a match-up of 5-0 teams, Lockett got behind the defense for a 58-yard scoring strike to cut NU's lead to 31-28 midway through the fourth quarter.

The following week against Colorado, Lockett had two big catches. Both came in the fourth quarter and were big for different reasons. The first was a leaping, one-handed grab where Lockett reached behind him and pulled the pass away from a defender. The other was on a fourth-and-15 from K-State's 31 that gained 44 yards and kept the game-tying drive alive.

"I've always known that I've had the ability to make those types of catches, but it just had never actually happened in a game," he said. "When I saw the game film I was amazed that I came down with the ball (on the one-hander). But I try to think that every ball is catchable."

Snyder believes the same thing when the ball is thrown in Lockett's direction. "He does the same things in practice," he said, "so it's hard to be surprised. But I'm certainly enamored by some of the catches he makes."

Lockett teamed with Coleman and Mitch Running to become the leading receiving trio in the conference. They caught 133 passes among them for 1,997 yards. Against Nebraska, they caught 23 balls for 348 yards. They were the second trio in league history to each catch at least 40 passes. With third-team all-America Coleman gone to the NFL, Lockett will be looked to for leadership on the receiving corps.

But any outside expectations will pale compared with his own. "I'd like to do a lot better than I did last year," he said. "I'd like to become the first 1,000-yard receiver in one season in Kansas State history. I'd like to lead the Big Eight in receiving. I'd also like to lead my team to the Orange Bowl.

"I have high expectations for Kansas State.

I practice with my teammates every day. I know what we have around us as a team and as coaches, and I really think those goals are within reach."

No doubt if he helps the Wildcats reach them, there will be a lot of people smiling.

Chad May focused in on a Big Eight record of 489 passing yards against Nebraska.

swarmed the field and tore down the goal posts, the players were "matter-of-fact," according to Snyder. "It wasn't at all like the Minnesota lockerroom. I think they had gained something in that Minnesota ballgame and it carried over to this one. In fact, I think as much as anything, the offense was probably a little subdued with the idea that they really hadn't performed as well as they possibly could, and that has a big impact on how people feel after a ballgame. You want it to be team thing. If one wins we all win, and if one loses, we all lose. Our players have been pretty good about that. If you win and didn't perform well as a player or as a coach, then there's a feeling that tugs at you that takes away some of the joy of a win. That's human nature. Our players and coaches are not removed from that."

But there was enough joy to go around, even for those who hadn't performed a peak effort.

Five-and-zero. It had a nice ring to it. It rang for the first time since 1934, and the Cats owned a school-best 10-game winning streak at home. It also set up one of the biggest games in school history – a road game at 5-0 Nebraska for an *inside track to the Orange Bowl.*

In '91, the Cats came to Lincoln and surprised the Huskers, losing a fourth-quarter lead and falling 38-31. In 1993, offense again was the story, in an all-Big Eight way.

Chad May threw 51 passes, completing 30 of them. He had touchdown throws of 70 and 58 yards. And he threw for 489 yards, the most ever by a quarterback in the Big Eight.

"Every time I was throwing, the guys were wide open," May said. "I can't say it was only I who did well. The line blocked, we rolled out a lot. We had to be one of the fastest teams in the nation. Nobody knew about us."

Despite the record yardage, the Wildcats did not win. Turnovers killed them. The

Cats had three turnovers, all either leading to NU scores or preventing KSU points. The first, a fumble at the Cats 21, led to Nebraska's first touchdown. J.J. Smith then took a short pass and raced 70 yards for the tying score, but Nebraska came right back and scored on Trumane Bell's 7-yard TD reception. Smith again tied it with a 3-yard scamper, but the Huskers scored two touchdowns to take a 28-14 lead with 3:12 to go in the half. The second drive was extended when the Cats were called for a personal foul that gave NU a first down when they otherwise would have had fourth-and-20.

Then came one of the big plays of the game. The Cats moved down to the Nebraska 3 with less than a minute left on May's 47-yard pass to Coleman. But on second down,

Mendez and the Wilcats were ready for the big time, battling 16th-ranked Colorado to a 16-16 tie.

Smith tried to hit May on the halfback option, but floated the pass and it was picked off by Tyrone Williams. If the pass were six inches longer, May might have caught it. Instead, the Huskers moved to the KSU 31 and Byron Bennett hit a career-long 48-yard field goal. It was a 10-point reversal that dampened the Cats' chances.

"That was one of four dramatic opportunities in the ballgame that really were instrumental in the outcome of the game. But again, they played well enough when they had to to win and we didn't play well enough when we had to," Snyder said.

The Cats rebounded quickly in the third quarter. Smith scored his third touchdown of the game, bringing the Cats to within 10. Then May hit Kevin Lockett with a 58-yard strike to make the score 31-28 early in the fourth.

But it was not enough. Nebraska responded with a seven-play drive to move back ahead by 10, and then held the Cats on fourth-and-goal from the four when Smith was stopped at the 2. Another long drive made the margin of victory 17.

After the game, Nebraska

Kevin Lockett's big gain on fourth down set up Tate Wright for the game-tying field field goal that split the uprights.

coach Tom Osborne gave the Cats quite a compliment when he said, "I'm glad to get out of that one, obviously. Somewhere down the line, they're going to beat somebody pretty good."

His kind words did nothing to soothe the hearts of the Cats. To a man, they felt they had beaten – or at least out-played – somebody pretty good. The Cornhuskers. Neujahr, a native of Nebraska, simply clinches up when talking about this game and the one that got away in 1991. "You've got to play sound ball all the way through, even though we set a lot of records," he said. "I think we lost that game. I'll believe that till the day I die. I think Kansas State lost that game."

The Colorado game the following week was the next opportunity to "beat somebody pretty good." The Buffaloes had demolished the Cats, 54-7, in 1992 and brought the No. 16 ranking into Manhattan with them. The Cats were just as good.

Tate Wright's 35-yard field goal into the wind with 21 seconds remaining gave the Wildcats and the Buffaloes a 16-16 tie.

Let's backtrack. CU owned the first half, outgaining the Cats, 239-36, in the half, but only led 9-0 on three Mitch Berger field goals. The Cats got rolling in the third, scoring their first offensive touchdown against the Buffs since 1989, when Coleman caught a tipped pass in the end zone. That's when Wright's streak of 31 straight extra points was ended by Shannon Clavelle. The Cats then took the lead on a May-to-Brad Seib pass with 9:57 left.

Freshman Kevin Lockett made his mark in the Big Eight with two big catches in the game. The first was a spectacular grab, when he reached back across his body and one-handed the ball, stealing it away from a surprised defender. "I saw that he was beyond the defensive back," May said. "I was rolling to my right and the guy was com-

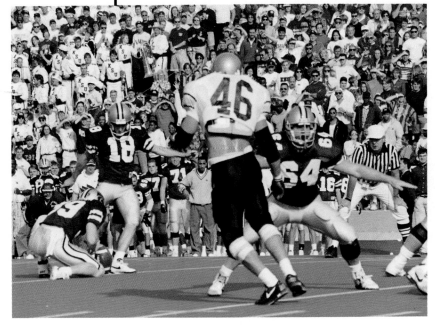

140

ing up in my face. I just tried to throw it as far as I could, because he was way out there. Then the defensive back was waiting for him. He came back for the ball and made the catch."

Lockett, as nonchalant in an interview as he seems to be on the field, at least until the ball is snapped, said, "I try to think that every ball is catchable."

With a four-point lead, the game was far from out of reach. The Buffs came right back and scored the go-ahead touchdown with 3:57 remaining after May's pass across the middle was tipped and intercepted by Dennis Collier. Had May's pass been three inches higher, the interception might not have occurred.

But the Wildcats didn't give up. They drove down the field to set up a game-tying field goal with 21 seconds left. Lockett's second big catch keyed the drive. With the Cats facing fourth-and-15 at their own 31, a rolling May found Lockett open over the middle.

Lockett's first instinct was to get the first down and run out of bounds. "When I looked up and saw how wide open I was, I just tried to get as many yards as I could and get out of bounds to save the clock," Lockett said. "In the huddle, we knew we had to do something if we wanted to win that game. We knew we had played too well to go out of that game a loser."

What they didn't know was that it already had been determined that a tie

After falling behind with less than four minutes remaining, the Cats executed a pressure-filled drive to the tying field goal in the final seconds.

would suffice. "That was the decision that I had made in advance of the ballgame, which I always do," Snyder said. "We were in a little different setting at that time than ever before. In the four years prior to this year, our theme always has been, 'We're playing to win, period.' That's a known entity, and our kids had become so ingrained in that. There was never a situation where a ballgame could have come down to a tie that it wasn't already cut and dried that we were going to play for the win until after we lost the Nebraska game."

The Cats went 62 yards to set up Wright's field goal, not an easy one into a stiff wind that had veered Berger's kick wide in the third quarter. Wright nailed it to set up tons of second-guessing for days to come. Not just from the media, or even the opposition.

"I've been real vocal ever since I've been here, and the newspaper people loved it, because I give them a lot of quotes," Mendez said. "Coach Snyder and I haven't always

All Mike Gundy could do was watch as the Oklahoma running game was bottled up at the line of scrimmage.

agreed on that. He was really hurt that I would question him publicly like that. He has no problem with me questioning him privately, but to do that publicly and give the people in the paper something to write about wasn't right, and I agreed that that wasn't right. I apologized to him and the team for doing that publicly.

"But in my heart, I still wanted to go for the win, and I told him that. I said, 'Coach, I still wanted to win this football game.' Looking back, I still wish we would have gone. That's just me. I wanted to win the game. I realize what it did for our program. I remember watching ESPN, and they made a huge thing about Kansas State tying."

Others, like Kenny McEntyre, didn't see the wisdom at the time, but changed their minds later on. "I didn't like the tie situation," he said. "That's just my opinion. I thought we should have gone for it, but it's over. Things worked out for the best. Looking back, it was the right decision, without a doubt. After the game, we were in the lockerroom looking at all the scenarios; tying the game was a good decision. It was not just difficult for the team to accept. It was difficult for Coach Snyder, too. He wanted to win; he didn't want to settle for a tie."

As John Butler prepared for mortuary school following his graduation from Kansas State, he certainly was prepared. He had heard all the jokes.

"It's a dying business," one person told him. "Yeah, but people still are dying to see you," he quickly responded. He also acknowledged that it wouldn't be easy. "There's stiff competition," he said.

It's not unlike his situation five years ago when he decided to walk on to the program at Kansas State. Most people thought he would be a stiff, just occupying space on the sideline. Unlike many of the players who excelled under Bill Snyder who were told not to go to Kansas State, John Butler was not advised to stay away because his talents would be wasted. He was told that he was incapable of playing at that level.

"I can remember people telling me not to go down there," he said. "They said, 'Stick around here where you can play. They really didn't think it was a good idea to go to K-State because they didn't think I'd play. They wanted me to stick around here or go to Kearney and have a chance to contribute right away to a program."

"Here" was Hastings, Nebraska, and more specifically, Hastings College, an NAIA school in Butler's home town. Kearney was the University of Nebraska at Kearney, a Division II school. He had no Division I opportunities.

"I came from a real small school," he said. "I graduated with 29 in my graduating class. I was only 185 pounds in high school, and not overly fast." That's a nice way of saying, "He's not big, but he sure is slow."

"Exactly," Butler said.

But he thought he could play Division I football. He believed his best chance was at Kansas State. "When I was growing up, they weren't very good," he said. "I knew the only way to go was up.

"Also, Coach Snyder came and said a lot of the things my high school coach had said about hard work and discipline. It worked in high school. It took us to the state playoffs for two years."

So Butler came to Kansas State and set out to earn a spot on the team. He built on his 6-2 frame, to the point where he finished his career at 225 pounds. He also finished as a two-year starter at defensive end.

"John got all his eggs in the right baskets," Snyder said. "He wanted to go to school here and he wanted the opportunity to play. He was a very well-rounded young man. He took good care of himself. He practiced hard and practiced smart. He also played hard and smart. He didn't make mistakes and played within himself extremely well."

Butler says he had to work hard, because he didn't have the physical skills of the other players at his position. "I don't know if it was because the guys who were in front of me came

And there were some who saw it Snyder's way from the beginning. "I'm not going to argue with Coach. I think he made the right decision," May said. "The way the season was going, he thought we were going to end up as the second-place team. I just don't think it should have come down to that. They got a cheap touchdown when the guy tried to sack me and hit the ball up in the air and they got the ball right down there. That's when they went in and scored. I'm not going to say I was happy at the time, but I think it was the right choice.

"I don't know if Coach Snyder cares what everybody thinks, but what if we had gone for it and missed it? Then he would have faced criticisms like, 'Why didn't you go for the field goal?' Either way, he was going to make a wrong decision."

Snyder didn't worry about the criticism. And he didn't want his players trying to figure out why certain decisions were made. "I don't try to put them in the position to have to think (about those situations), because they've got so many decisions to make on the field," Snyder said. "The reason behind it was we still had a chance to be in a coalition bowl with tying that ballgame. Had we lost the ballgame, then we would not have had the opportunity to be

here on scholarships and were a lot faster than I was," he said. "They held some of the records on the testing board. I just never really thought that I could compete with them because they were a lot quicker than I was. Hopefully I made up for it by playing smart. I just thought that if I could do the job I was told to do, and do it right close to 100 percent of the time and not make any mistakes, then that was my big advantage."

Butler's story is a good example of how "The Wildcat's Fourteen Goals for Success" can be used. "During the North Texas game (in 1989), Eric Gallon told me, 'We're never going to win unless we start becoming good people,'" he said. "My high school coach really preached the discipline part and working hard and being physically tough and not complaining. As the years went on, I don't think you so much remember the 14 goals. You just do them.

"More than anything is the self discipline part. That's the one I really bought into. I believe strongly in that, doing what you're supposed to do and having the will power to say, 'I'm going to do this,' and just get it done. In terms of school, it really helped you out. You'd want to go out and do something, but you had that test the next day. It helped you make the right decision."

Butler finished his career, not only as a two-year starter, but as a team captain. "He was an excellent role model and our players had great respect for him," Snyder said. "That's why they selected him as a captain."

Quite a finish for someone who wasn't supposed to be able to play at this level. Now, when he returns to those same people in Hastings who tried to convince him that he couldn't play Division I football, he quickly hearkens back. "Several people have come up to me and said, 'Great job, you had a great year,'" he said. "I think, 'Thank you, but I remember when you told me to not go down there, you thought I should stick around here.' But I don't say that to them."

Even if he is just "dying" to say it.

143

in a coalition bowl. We kept it alive with the tie."

It didn't get the Cats second place in the conference because of a loss to Iowa State two weeks later. But the tie enabled the Cats to earn the best record against the "Big Three" that any other conference school had achieved in the previous 10 years.

The situation also made it look like a good choice. The Cats were faced with fourth-and-three with less than 30 seconds remaining and no timeouts. Even if they had reached the first down, no easy task, there would be little time to gain the final 15 yards for the touchdown against a nationally ranked defense.

The tie also got the Cats into the national rankings for the first time since 1970 at

Chad May had plenty of time to pick apart the OU defense and find receivers like Mitch Running to build a 21-point lead.

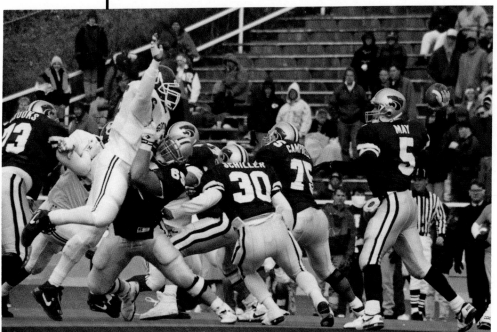

No. 25. That made the game against Oklahoma on Homecoming the first game *ever played* at KSU Stadium between two ranked teams.

Despite the national ranking and two close games against the nation's elite teams, not everybody was convinced. John Rohde of *The Daily Oklahoman*, wrote the week prior to the game, "A team winless since October 9 has rocketed into the Top 25 for the first time in 23 years. I don't believe it. Nor do I understand it. (The Wildcats) tied Colorado last week, but the Buffs viewed KSU as an off week sandwiched between OU and NU and got burned. They're vastly improved, up-and-coming and on-the-rise. But I'm still not a believer. If KSU is the 25th-best team in the country, Division I-A football is in a world of hurt right now."

Rohde was wrong. The Cats weren't the 25th-best team in the country. They were much better. They proved that by defeating the No. 14-ranked Sooners.

The Cats controlled from the opening gun. They led 7-0 at halftime and 21-0 before the Sooners scored a late touchdown to avoid the shutout.

The Cats used to be everybody's Homecoming guest. But this win was the fourth straight win for KSU on its own Homecoming, and against a team that it hadn't beaten since 1970, the domination of a very good Oklahoma team showed just how far the program had come.

The Wildcats really didn't play at the top of their game. They turned over the ball four times and were outgained, 393-330. They just were better than the Sooners. It was a methodical beating. K-State sacked Cale Gundy four times and gave up 206 of the yards after the 21-0 lead was established.

"It was just a tremendous victory for our constituency," Snyder said. "It was something really special to them. In our lockerroom, it was a very matter-of-fact attitude after that ballgame. Our guys knew that they had not beaten Oklahoma in their tenure here, but it was just that indication that they knew that if they played well and did the right things that they could win that ballgame."

The victory vaulted the Cats to No. 18, their second-highest ranking ever. And it was secured early enough that Mitch Holthus, the excitable "Voice of the Wildcats" who became famous for his "Big, Big, Big..." calls after important victories, could prepare his game-ending comments ahead of time.

"It's over! This game's over!" Holthus rasped into the microphone as the final seconds ticked off the clock. "This ballgame's over, and you listen to me closely! Listen to me closely! Because for the first time since Exodus, Chapter 14, the Red Sea has been parted, and Pharaoh's Sooner chariots have been swallowed up! Because Bill 'Moses' Snyder says, 'Let my people go from 23 years of Sooner bondage!

"So wind it on up for Kansas State. Because for K-State, winning, 21-7, over Oklahoma it's a big, big, big, big, big, big, big, big, big, big Kansas State victory over Oklahoma."

That's 10 bigs, for those of you keeping score at home. Did he plan it?

"It was planned," Holthus said. "It was planned to be used at Nebraska. It was ready to go at Nebraska, because I really thought Kansas State had an excellent chance to win that game, and that would have been parting the Red Sea as well. It would have been the first time since '68. But after their hopes were dashed in the fourth quarter, it went right back in the brief case waiting for another day, and that day was Oklahoma."

Holthus earned national recognition for the call. The recording was picked up by a radio station in southern California, which put it on the wires, where it was picked up by newspapers across the country, including the *Miami Herald* and the *St. Paul (Minnesota) Pioneer Press.*

"I suppose when I wrote that, it was an attention-getting maneuver," Holthus said. "But I feel very good that the program got a lot of attention by it. Someone may have thought, 'Gosh, Kansas State is doing something in football.' That might have been the first indication across the country that it was happening. Then they start to follow this team; they see them in the Top-20 rankings. Then they see them on ESPN in the Copper Bowl, and they're going, 'Whoa.' If that did that for one or two people across the country, it's worth it."

Snyder appreciated Holthus' enthusiasm, but was uncomfortable with the comparison. "It certainly is a category in which I don't belong," he said. "Mitch has a way with words and he can get the fans excited, but I'm just as human as the next guy."

The Cats ended their three-game stretch against the "Big Three" riding high. It was the first time since Colorado had returned to national prominence in 1985 that a Big Eight team had done as well as Kansas State (1-1-1) against the trio. But there still remained room for improvement. "The 1-1-1 probably was satisfying to some people," Snyder said, "but to many of us, it was disappointing. You look back and you envision how far away we were from 3-0-0."

The Cats headed into the home stretch 6-1-1 overall, 2-1-1 in the Big Eight, and in prime position to finish second or third in the conference. They were one win away from clinching a bowl berth and three wins against sub-.500 teams away from possibly qualifying for a New Year's Day bowl game.

But the Cats quickly learned a lesson about being overconfident, suffering a 27-23 loss to Iowa State. Opinions differ on why it happened, but nobody disputes the fact that it brought the Cats crashing to Earth.

"I'd like to have that one back. I think everybody would," Neujahr said. "Overconfident? Maybe. Coming off the 'Big Three' having great success, going into what everybody calls the smaller three of our season, we got off the bus (Friday night) and saw the snow fly. It was cold and miserable. Every so often the weather played to our advantage. I think the weather played to our disadvantage this time."

Snyder said, "That's a very strong indication of a mental let-down. We weren't as tough as we needed to be," he said.

The game never appeared comfortable for the Cats, although they did lead 17-6 late in the third. Following two Ty Stewart field goals, the Cats took the lead on a 1-yard

The world of sports is the world of cliches. "You've got to play them one game at a time," "It's not over 'til the Fat Lady sings" and "Defense wins championships" are as common as ABCs and Xs and Os. In this world of "giving 110 percent," the living embodiment of "You can't coach speed" is Thomas Randolph.

Randolph played his final year of high school ball in Manhattan. His breathtaking speed was his trademark for the state-champion Indians during his senior season. But no major colleges gave him a chance to play football. He was recruited by several schools to run track, but that just didn't fit into his plans. "My dream was to play college football in the Big Eight," he said. "I was heavily recruited as a track athlete, so I said, 'I'm going to use track to get into Big Eight football.'"

The coaching staff recognized that Randolph's speed would allow him to be an outstanding cornerback, a position at which he had a chance to help the program and get on the field quicker, so they switched him to cornerback. Randolph was pleased with the switch because it would allow him to use his speed and athleticism, something he says is his strongest

suit. "I haven't played at defensive back for a long time," he said. "I still have a lot of learning to do. My best football is yet to come. In college I used my speed a lot to help me in the things that I couldn't do, because I knew nobody could run by me."

Snyder had the benefit of knowing the other coach had to figure out how to beat Randolph. "Tommy could line up on top of somebody, and the quarterback would feel hard pressed to try to throw the ball over the top, just because of the knowledge that Tommy could run so well," Snyder said. "It appeared to be a futile attempt to do so. Being on defense was good for him."

Randolph was drafted in the second round of the NFL Draft by the New York Giants, the fifth cornerback taken in the draft. He knows the next level will have more guys who can compete with him on the track as well as the football field. "My coach (in the pros) is trying to instill in me now (that I won't be able to blow by people). He said, 'Every day you're going to go against fast people. You've got to learn how to play technique and play more sound mentally.'"

Even though Randolph did not have the football skills that Snyder

looked for, he made up for that with his eagerness to learn. "I was going to be one of those people who would work hard, even though we were losing," he said. "I was going to try to find some kind of improvement that was going on during the games. We had to find something to keep stepping on, and we'd finally get there. Soon we did."

Hard work was a trademark of Randolph's at Manhattan High, where he teamed in the secondary with Maurice Benson, another speedy defensive back, who went to Missouri. Benson was more highly recruited than Randolph, but they had numerous discussions about playing college ball together. "Maurice and I came out the same year," Randolph said. "He said, 'K-State is not going to win; I'm going to go to a winning program.' So I said, 'Missouri is not a winning program. You just want to leave Manhattan, is that it?' He said, 'No, it's the program.' And I said, 'It's a Big Eight school. I'm going to believe in Coach Snyder, and I'm going to believe in the people.'"

While Benson, and the Tigers, struggled, Randolph flourished. He was a three-time all-America in indoor track in the 55-meter dash, and was named a second-team all-America at

dive by Smith. It stood 7-6 at the half.

Mendez forced Iowa State quarterback Bob Utter to fumble on the first play of the third quarter, which led to a Tate Wright field goal. Following a Randolph interception, the Cats drove 45 yards in six plays to take a 17-6 lead. But the Cats still seemed to be struggling. They gained just 51 yards on the ground for the game, compared with 222 for Iowa State.

In the fourth quarter, the tide changed. The

cornerback in 1993. The *NFL Draft Report* called him, "the finest player to perform at this spot in the past decade. All doubters should go back and watch how he dominated receiver Charles Johnson (of Colorado)... This is one player who will be spending quite a few years playing in the Pro Bowl."

That same magazine had glowing reports on two of Randolph's teammates in the secondary – Jaime Mendez and Kenny McEntyre. Together with Kitt Rawlings, the quartet formed the "Secondary to None."

"We went to the scouting combines and we were telling everybody, 'We're the best secondary in the country,'" Randolph said. "They said, 'How is that?' We said, 'Because we allowed fewer touchdowns than anybody in the country.' They would say, 'I heard you were fast and Jaime could hit.' We had three all-Big Eight performers in the secondary. I was like, 'Can anybody else say they did that?' They were like, 'I got all...' I said, 'Well, that's you, where is your supporting cast?'

"Coach (Bobby) Stoops would

say, 'Do you want to be the greatest? That's what you've got to do.'"

Mendez said his job was easier with Randolph and McEntyre at the corners and Rawlings at strong safety. "It got to the point where we knew how good we were," he said. "That's kind of scary when you have a secondary that is cocky like that. But we could back it up, and we always did. It was real fun, because I'd say, 'I'm going to go up here and try to knock this guy out. If I miss him, I've got Tom and Kenny and Kitt to back me up. I know one of them is going to make the tackle.' All of us took our turns taking risks like that and most of the time it paid off."

With McEntyre and Mendez joining him in the pros in the fall of 1994, Randolph is looking forward to keeping in touch with the guys he joined in the backfield, especially Mendez who signed with the Giants' rival, Philadelphia. "Yes, it's going to be fun looking at him on the sidelines," he said. "(Giants Stadium) is only 45 min-

utes away, so I'm pretty sure we're going to keep in touch and be real close. It's going to be great. We can always call and say, 'I saw you get burned. I saw you miss that tackle.' We're going to be on each other's backs still, just like we were in college."

A quick check of history bodes well for Randolph fans. He won the state championship in his fourth year of high school, and he won a Copper Bowl ring in his final year of college ball. Maybe there's still time to place that bet on the Giants for Super Bowl XXXI.

Cyclones streaked – literally – to 21 unanswered points in the final 15 minutes to take control of the game. A fan raced onto the field wearing nothing but a smile, and on the next play, Iowa State seemed to come to life. "It wasn't so cold he couldn't do that," Snyder joked.

On the next play, Calvin Branch raced 19 yards for what was the key play of ISU's scoring drive. Kansas State could not sustain their next drive and the Cyclones got the ball back. They had third-and-six at the KSU 49 when one of those "three-inch" plays bit the Cats. Todd Doxzon, who had replaced Utter, threw a pass over the middle that was batted by K-State defensive lineman Kelly Greene. Center Tony Booth caught the deflection and rumbled 8 yards for a first down. Combine those three inches with the six at Nebraska on Smith's option pass and the three against Colorado on the deflected interception, and it is easy to see how the Cats were "less than two feet from the Orange Bowl," by Snyder's quick calculation.

"They got some momentum when they got that little tipped pass," Snyder said. "All of a sudden we're on our heels. The momentum has changed, we can't get the brakes put on and it's over. There was a tremendous price to pay for that lesson."

The Cyclones scored to take a 20-17 lead. The Cats went four-and-out on their next possession and the Cyclones took advantage of the short field with a four-play drive to ice the game. J.J. Smith's long run after a short catch made the final score respectable.

"You have to take the bad with the good," Snyder said. "It's a lesson. Aren't they all? It's a reminder of the same things that have plagued the growth of the program from time to time. It's taking something for granted. It's trying to take short cuts.

"Unfortunately, our players read more than they needed to read. Coach (Jim) Walden told the press that this team (K-State) has played all those other ballgames and has played so hard and so well during that time, that they can't keep that up, can't stay at that same emotional peak all the time. Well, we had gone 4 1/2 years saying that we don't have the luxury of picking and choosing when our emotional games are. We've got to do it every single time out or anybody can beat us and we proved the point. We've not been good enough just to be methodical."

The loss left the Cats still one win short of qualifying for a bowl game heading into the home finale against Missouri. The fact that the Wildcats had a rancid taste in their mouths from the previous week and that the game would be the final time Snyder's original recruiting class would wear the home purples made the contest very emotional.

"I remember not wanting to leave the field that day, the last time I'd ever play there," Mendez said. "I remember crying before the game. Almost every senior was crying together. It was just a real emotional day for all of us."

"The group of seniors had been through so much together in the last five years," added Neujahr.

Apparently the emotions kept the Wildcats from playing their best. They assumed a 10-0 lead at halftime, but fell behind, 13-10, after two third-quarter Missouri scores. Then the offense got in gear. Three long passes, including a 27-yard strike to Coleman, and the Cats were back in front. The Cats began their next possession at their own 35. On first down, MU jumped off-sides and Neujahr snapped the ball. May took one step back and fired a pass to Coleman, who juked his man and raced 65 yards untouched.

Cats 24, Tigers 13. Game over.

Missouri fumbled at their 5 on their next possession and May dived in for the clinching score with 5:30 left.

"This was probably the first time they were sensing the outside world's expectations," Snyder said. "All of a sudden, now they were upon them. What everybody was interested in was a bowl game."

When it was clinched, it was more of a relief than sheer joy for the players. "It definitely was a sense of relief, because I don't think that anybody wanted to go to Oklahoma State with our backs against the wall, having to win to go to a bowl game," Neujahr said. "Stillwater is a tough place to win in itself. Anytime you play on the road in the Big Eight, it's tough. We didn't need to do that, so it definitely was a relief."

For Holthus, who had missed the bowl game in 1982, and had seen an NCAA rule keep the Cats out of a bowl in 1991, the victory was special. "The play I remember was Chad reaching across the goal line for a touchdown," he said. "It is an unspectacular play from a highlight standpoint, but I remember the feeling I had, and it was an incredible feeling, the feeling of, 'It's going to happen. We're going.'"

While the Cats had clinched a bowl invitation and had closed their second straight undefeated home season, there was plenty to play for in the regular-season finale at Oklahoma State. (That *regular* season sounded pretty good to Wildcats fans.) The Cats could clinch third place in the conference with a win, assure themselves of the most wins in 62 years, and assure themselves of a Top-20 national ranking at season's end.

"I think for us not to have been as competitive as possible for a third place finish in the conference as opposed to a fourth place would not have been expecting a great deal out of ourselves, which would be contrary to what our team goals would be," Snyder said. "Granted, there wasn't the same pressure that presented itself in the Missouri ballgame. It wasn't a matter of having to win to go to a bowl game. But there were a lot of other things that were still at stake that should have made that equally as important as the Missouri ballgame."

The end zone awaited Chad May as he prepared to clinch K-State's second bowl bid in history with a victory over Missouri.

Apparently the team wasn't quite convinced. Although they led 14-0 in the second quarter and 14-7 at halftime, the Wildcats couldn't put away the game. They had a chance in the third quarter but May was intercepted in the end zone.

The Cowboys tied the game with 8:07 left when a broken play got fixed. Daryl "Boogie" Johnson ran the halfback option to the sideline, where he nearly stepped out of

Coleman had a key catch and a pass-interference call on the thrilling game-winning drive against Oklahoma State.

bounds. But right before getting hit, he threw to Rafael Denson, who fell into the end zone for the tying score.

The Cats still couldn't move the ball and Lawson Vaughn booted a career-best 43-yard field goal with just 58 seconds left. The scoreboard at Lewis Field read, "Gotta Love It!"

It didn't look real good for the Cats, unless you happened to be standing in the huddle on the sidelines before the Cats took the field at their 20.

"Kevin walked up to me and I winked at him and said, 'We're going to do it,'" May said.

In a drive reminiscent of the one against North Texas in 1989, May moved the Cats 80 yards in 41 seconds with no timeouts and hit Brad Seib seven yards deep in the end zone for the winning score.

That same scoreboard read, "Drive Safely."

"We walked out there and got an illegal procedure penalty right away and then we just rolled," May said. "The defense softened up a little bit on us. It went so fast, I can't explain it. Pop, pop, pop, and we're already down there. Then they got the pass interference call down on the goal line. I knew we were going to score right when we got down there. I knew what Coach was going to call and that's the play that came in. They had no way of defending it. We just went nuts after the score."

Holthus came into the game with laryngitis and lost what was left of his voice on the final drive. Here's another famous call: "Out of the shotgun, May, back to throw, shifts the pocket right. Now fires a pass that is caught by Lockett out of bounds at the 33-yard line. Stops the clock. It is a first down.

"K-State will use the shotgun. Two receivers left, there's a flanker right. J.J. Smith is just to the left of May. May says he cannot hear the snap count. Back to throw is May. Rolling left...still rolling left. Now fires a pass to the far sideline, caught by

Coleman. He makes the catch and is out of bounds at the OSU 49-yard line. A 24-yard pass play. Thirty-eight seconds left to go in the game, 17-14, Oklahoma State. A great throw by May and another good catch by Coleman to the boundary to stop the clock.

"Two receivers to the right and one to the left. On first down, out of the shotgun snap, May moving right, being chased. Now launches the football down the near side-line. Caught by Lockett and out of bounds at the 22-yard line! Again, it appeared that Delvin Miles was in a position to make the interception. Much like the Oklahoma game, Lockett comes back to the football and makes the catch, out of bounds to stop the clock at the OSU 22-yard line with 31 seconds left in the game.

"K-State, out of the shotgun, first-and-10 at the OSU 22-yard line. Back to throw, May throws near side to Running, (who) makes the catch out of bounds at the 17-yard line, it's a gain of 5.

"K-State on second down-and-six at the Pokes' 17, now they're throwing for the end zone. K-State throwing deep and the pass is incomplete but a flag thrown in the end zone! Andre Coleman was trying to make the catch but Oklahoma State will be called for pass interference in the end zone. K-State was trying to run the deep corner route to Andre Coleman, and the pass (was) broken up. They move the ball to the 2-yard line.

"Brian Rees and Dederick Kelly in for Kansas State. Rod Schiller was injured earlier. Twenty-one seconds left to go in the game. First-and-goal K-State at the Oklahoma State 2-yard line. No timeouts left for K-State. Play-action fake by May. He's throwing for the end zone, pass is caught by Seib! Touchdown! He caught it 9 yards deep in the end zone off the play-action! K-State takes the lead, with 17 seconds left to go in the game! What a drive!"

"I've been coaching for a long time," Snyder said after the game. "I've been around a lot of great quarterbacks. I've seen a lot of come-from-behind victories, and I've seen a lot of great two-minute drives. But nothing matches the one Chad engineered today. It was truly a fantastic performance."

Six months barely dampened his enthusiasm. "The sideline was very, very confident," he said. "The defensive players were confident that the offense could do it. Nobody had given up the ship. A lot of very positive things came out of that. Chad did a nice job. It was his play selection for the most part, with the help of his receivers.

"You wouldn't be a very good coach if you were totally caught up in the emotion of everything or if you were frightened. But it doesn't mean that your heart doesn't beat a little harder than it does at other times. I'm not inhuman."

The Cats finished the season in improbable fashion. A four-year sweep of the Cowboys, third place in the Big Eight and the most wins in a three-year stretch since 1910-12. But most importantly, for the first time since any of the current players or coaches had been at K-State, the season wasn't over when the final gun had sounded.

COPPER BOWL
TURNING COPPER INTO GOLD

Total domination.

That is probably the easiest way to describe Kansas State's 52-17 victory over Wyoming in the 1993 Copper Bowl. The Cats outgained the Cowboys, 502-302. They scored on offense, defense and special teams. They ran wild on the Cowboys' run defense and stopped the pass-happy Cowboys through the air. Kansas State's all-America wide receiver Andre Coleman was named the game's offensive MVP with 283 total yards. Wyoming's all-America wide receiver Ryan Yarborough, the NCAA's career yardage leader was held to just 72 yards receiving. It was his second worst game of the year, barely half his season's average.

When the final seconds ticked off the clock of this duel, all that remained were the Cowboy-shaped chalk drawings on the sidewalk.

"In my five years, without a doubt that's the best game that Kansas State's ever put together on the field," senior center Quentin Neujahr said. "We had the total package, offense, defense, special teams. We couldn't have asked for a better way to do it. We went into that game saying, 'No matter what it takes, no matter what goes on, we're not going to lose.'

"We were out there sending a message to the entire United States of America saying, 'Kansas State is for real. We're a top 20 team and we deserve to be there. If you're not convinced after this game, then you're not going to be convinced.'"

Kansas State dominated from the outset – of the bowl week – not just the game. A swarm of Wildcats fans, conservatively estimated at 15,000, turned the Blue-and-Red Wildcat town of Tucson, Arizona, into a Purple Wildcat town.

"I worked at the La Paloma Hotel last year

Coleman's two touchdown dashes sandwiched around halftime blew open a close game.

153

where Washington State had a contingent," said George Brownlee, a Tucson resident and a Copper Bowl Foundation volunteer. "The Washington State people were nice to work with, but these K-State people have been fabulous. The enthusiasm is great and they have been extremely friendly, not to mention the economic impact the city will see because K-State is bringing a lot of people."

K-Staters came by bus (88 of them were chartered by the alumni association), plane (16 DC-10s brought purple followers) and car (an uncountable train of personal vehicles made every rest stop between Manhattan and Tucson a

The fans came in large numbers to watch the Cats dismantle the potent offense of Christopherson (34) and Wyoming.

friendly place for Wildcats).

"I think people (in Tucson) became enamored with Kansas State people, because there were so many of them there," Snyder said. "There was a common bond of being Wildcats. I don't think it had anything to do with the teams, because I don't think anybody felt that Wyoming wasn't a very capable football team."

Once in Tucson, the Wildcats faithful turned the town into West Manhattan. Every store, hotel and tourist site was a rallying point for K-Staters. "I think there were closer

to 25,000 K-Staters," Neujahr said. "I don't care what the record says, I think there were closer to 25,000. Everywhere you looked it was purple. It was like Tucson was turning into Manhattan, Kansas. It definitely made us feel great."

When the official functions began, even the locals were impressed with the KSU turnout. *Arizona Daily Star* columnist Greg Hansen called Kansas State a "perfect fit with perfect timing" for the Copper Bowl.

"People in purple were everywhere," he wrote. "Thousands of them. Tailgating even before noon in small pockets of people all over the UA campus. Taking their seats in Arizona Stadium 75 minutes before kickoff....Kids waiting for Christmas."

"The highways were lined with Wildcats fans all the way from Oklahoma, honking and cheering for KSU," wrote Sarah Tully, also of the *Daily Star*. "The usual sea of University of Arizona red on the UA mall before games was replaced with a stream of purple and some gold speckles, the respective colors of bowl competitors Kansas State University and the University of Wyoming."

When the K-State athletic department held a rally the day before the game, more than 3,000 people attended. It is hard to say exactly how many, but the ballroom was

It's pretty appropriate that Jaime Mendez ended his career leading Kansas State in interceptions. After all, he was quite a steal himself.

Mendez came to Kansas State from Youngstown, Ohio, where he played linebacker and fullback at Cardinal Mooney High School. The defensive coordinator for Mooney was Ron Stoops, the father of K-State assistant coaches Bobby and Mike Stoops. While it sounds like the familial connection secured Mendez's talents for K-State, it actually was the fact that the Wildcats were competing for Mendez by themselves. Mendez was considered too slow to play in the defensive backfield in major college ball, and was too small to play linebacker.

"I was a B-list player," Mendez said. "They'll take you if someone else doesn't sign. I was like that for a lot of Big Ten schools. I don't know exactly how much of a steal you could call me at that time. I thought I was a really good player. I was an all-state player in high school, but I seem to have had the same problem I have going to this level (the pros): a lot of people thought I was a tad too slow or a tad too small. I just always thought I had the heart.

"It makes me feel good to know that the program did what it did and I

personally became the best in the country at my position, because a lot of people did overlook me. They didn't see it in me, but I always saw it in myself."

Bobby Stoops, who began recruiting Mendez for Kent State and then went after him after he took a position on Bill Snyder's new staff at Kansas State, saw something the other recruiters didn't see in Mendez. "Right away, I was able to see his quickness, speed and intelligence," Stoops said. "And from my father, I knew he was a person of great character who had a great work ethic."

Mendez also saw something different in K-State, a school in the throes of a 27-game winless streak. "He (Snyder) is a real good spokesman," Mendez said. "He has a way of conveying his message real well. He just pretty much sold us on the fact that he was going to make the greatest turnaround in college football history. That's what he sold all of us, that first group of guys he brought in. He told us, 'I'm positive this is going to be the greatest story ever in college football, and I would like you to be a part of it. I'm only choosing certain players to do that. I know that you're not a highly recruited player, but I think you're the type of player who would fit in here.'"

Mendez felt wanted, and felt a

security blanket in Stoops, so he packed his bags and headed to Kansas State. It was a decision he regretted quickly. Several times in his first year, he had his bags packed and was ready to head back to Youngstown. "Eric Wolford and I had plans to leave three or four different times," he said. "But they talked us into staying every time. When it came down to it, it was my parents. My dad told me, 'Give it a year. If it doesn't work out after one year, I'll go with any decision you want, but don't leave before you spend one entire school year there. We were competitive in three or four games, and that helped a lot. The fact that they stuck me in the starting lineup in the spring gave me a lot of hope for the future."

Mendez started his redshirt freshman year as the nickel back and backup at all four secondary positions. "I've never seen a player like that who not only had the ability to play both corners and safety," Stoops said, "but the really impressive thing is that he understands them, too." Intercepting six passes, he earned Big Eight Newcomer of the Year honors.

Four years later, Mendez can look back on a tremendous amount of success. He says that the fifth-year seniors of 1993 have the best perspective, having

supposed to hold 3,000 people and the fire marshal was not among those standing in the aisles.

"Kansas State people have proven that they travel well," Snyder said. "That certainly will benefit us when we are in a position to have an opportunity to compete in future post-season bowl games. That will be a plus for us,

come through all the hardship of the early years to be bowl champions. "It's hard to put into words how satisfying 1993 was," he said. "I think only the fifth-year seniors understand what had gone on here. It's something we all dreamed about."

The individual honors were beyond Mendez's dreams. He said he always dreamed of being all-Big Eight, and even hoped to be an all-America selection, but he was surprised how quickly the accolades came.

He finished his career as the all-time K-State interception leader with 15, including a school-record four in one game against Temple in 1992. His 313 tackles rank ninth in school history, second among defensive backs. He was a semifinalist for both the Thorpe Award, given annually to the nation's best defensive back, and *Football News'* National Defensive Player of the Year his senior year. He was a three-time first-team all-Big Eight selection and K-State's second consensus all-America in the

past two years.

But the numbers alone don't really tell the story for Mendez, much like the numbers alone can't summarize the turnaround he helped happen. The *NFL Draft Report* said of Mendez, "There is not a more aggressive or instinctive player in the nation. The only thing that will stop him from being an All-Pro is if the NFL gives up playing football. In my 15 years in the industry, I have never seen a defensive back control the outcome of a game like this guy can."

Instinctive. It's a good way to describe Mendez. He came to Kansas State because his instincts told him that he could believe Snyder. "It's been the greatest five years of my life," he said. "I'm so thankful to God and my family that I didn't quit, that I stayed here and all this came about.

"I live and die for this place now. I'll be one of the biggest K-State fans ever. Even though I might not be able to be here all the time, I'll always be rooting for them."

because it's evidence that we'll have an excellent following. I was happy as I could be that so many people had such great enjoyment out of the whole package."

When the Copper Bowl parade passed through the streets of Tucson the day of the game, more than 30,000 people watched, 10,000 more than the number who watched the previous year.

The game itself attracted a crowd of 49,075, bettering the mark set the previous year of 40,826.

"I think the big difference is the way we were treated," Neujahr said. "Now we were Nebraska (regarding the treatment from the Coca Cola Bowl in 1992). I really think Wyoming got the shaft. I really do, because everything that we did as a function and group, was centered around Kansas State. If they had a function, they'd come to our resort. From what I was told, we got the nicer resort of the two. We got all the little things that made them say, 'We wanted you. We appreciate you. We think you're the kings.'"

Walking onto the field before the game, there were poignant feelings, especially for the fifth-year seniors who had been through the entire turnaround. "It was like we were watching a movie," Thomas Randolph said. "Jaime (Mendez) and I said it was like somebody just wrote it down and knew how the ending was going to be, even if the characters didn't know. We had talked about it as freshmen and as sophomores. We said, 'We're going to leave with a ring.'

"Coach Snyder, Jaime and I were the last ones out of the lockerroom. He told us, 'This is what you came for; this is what I've tried to instill in you. Please tell our freshmen and sophomores how you got here.' Jaime and I started crying before the game. We were just tearing. Then we got out there and saw all the K-State fans, and we were pumped up. We weren't going to beat them by one. We were going to beat them thoroughly."

The game did not start the way the Purple Haze had wanted it to. On Wyoming's opening possession, Yarborough had a catch-and-run for

J.J. Smith and the Wildcats had numerous opportunities to practice their end zone celebrations.

159

an apparent 52-yard touchdown, but a false-start penalty negated it.

"We gambled a little bit on that play," Mendez said. "Coach kind of put everybody up on the line. Usually I'm always the safety valve, but on that play we were all on the line of scrim-

The story of the turnaround of the Kansas State football program under Bill Snyder has been called a real-life version of the movie *Hoosiers*. In the movie, Gene Hackman takes a bad, small-town Hickory High School basketball team from its moribund status all the way to the top. Hackman was tough on his players, but he instilled that toughness, and a confidence in themselves, that allowed them to overcome great obstacles to win a state championship.

When Snyder arrived at Kansas State, he was facing the biggest odds in the history of college football. He demanded a lot from his players, but drove them to accomplish far more than anyone thought possible. From a 30-game winless streak to a Top-20 finish and a Copper Bowl victory, Snyder's troops were changing the status of Kansas State football from big-time loser to champion.

Just like in the movie, where Hackman had Jimmy Chitwood, an immensely talented player who struggled early in the season and later came back to be a hero, Snyder had Andre Coleman. Coleman was expected to be a leader for the 1993 Wildcats, but he had trouble catching the ball during the spring and even into fall practice. But he turned things around and finished his career as the offensive MVP at the Copper Bowl and the MVP of the Hula

Bowl, the premier all-star game for college seniors.

Oh yeah. Coleman also was a state champion for Hickory High. *Really.*

Coleman is from Hermitage, Pennsylvania, where he rushed for more than 3,700 yards and scored 67 touchdowns in his final two seasons. He led Hickory to the 2A state football championship his senior year, when he scored 37 touchdowns and was named the small-school Player of the Year in the state. The names of schools that came calling at his door roll off the tongue like a Who's Who in eastern college football – Penn State, Pittsburgh, West Virginia, Georgia Tech.

But all those schools wanted him either as a receiver or a defensive back. At 5-10, 170 pounds, he was told he was too small to play running back. But Snyder told him he could try his hand at running back if he wanted to.

"Everybody in Pennsylvania thought I was the dumbest guy to go to K-State," he said. "Being Player of the Year, every-

body pretty much assumed that I would go to Pitt or Penn State. Pitt was dead, smack in the middle of the city, and I didn't want that. Penn State wanted me to play defense. Tony Dorsett and Eric Dickerson were my favorite running backs and I wanted to be like them."

Kansas State also offered him the opportunity to play his first year, something the other schools did not, so he chose to head to Manhattan. "One thing Coach Snyder said to me that was appealing, and it kind of raised my eyebrows, was, 'We'd love to have you here, but we're an up-and-coming program and we're going to win with you or without you,'" Coleman said. "It was kind of a cocky statement coming from a 1-10 team, but it just showed how much confidence he had in his coaching staff and the way he saw the future."

It didn't take long for Coleman to realize that he wasn't big enough to play running back in the Big Eight, so he switched to receiver. Certainly, he could have had second thoughts about the

mage. Kenny (McEntyre) hadn't had the feel for Yarborough yet. We should have waited a little longer 'til Kenny knew the guy's moves. He didn't know his moves yet and just got beat. We learned real quick."

With the reprieve, the KSU defense stiffened and allowed only a Taylor Sorenson field goal. The Cats responded with a 68-yard drive for a touchdown, highlighted by J.J. Smith's 30-yard run. When Smith plunged in from the 2, the Cats had the lead to stay. With KSU's offensive firepower, the team was confident that nobody could outscore them in a shoot-out.

"I was confident in our offense all year," Coleman said. "It wasn't because it was against a team that gave up a lot of points. I think if we'd played any other team on that given night, we still would have scored a lot of points."

The Cats' defense was a bit incensed by the talk of a 100-point game, and they were determined not to let it happen. "I was telling the media after the game, I don't know where their coaches watch tapes," McEntyre said. "The most we ever gave up was 48

programs he rejected when he ended up playing the position they wanted him to play. But Coleman never doubted his decision.

"It crossed my mind that if I had known I was going to play receiver, maybe I would have gone to another school," he said. "But I was happy with the coaching staff and I was happy with the guys on my team. I saw the turn-around coming and I wanted to be a part of it. I easily could have gone to Penn State and stepped right into a winning program. But in the long run, I probably wouldn't have gotten the recognition that I got for the simple fact that they already have a rich tradition in football. By coming here and helping this turnaround, I think I got more publicity."

He also got the opportunity to learn from a talented tandem of receivers. Michael Smith and Frank Hernandez were the incumbents when Coleman arrived, and Smith immediately took Coleman under his wing. "He taught me a lot about the receiver position," Coleman said. "Those two years I had with him were a big plus. I don't think anybody wanted me to do as well as Michael did, as much as Michael did. He wanted me to do very well.

"Michael saw talent in me a long time ago. He always told me, 'Andre, you've got the talent to play.' At the time I didn't believe him. I didn't think I had the

talent to play at the next level. But I guess when someone tells you over and over, you start to believe it. He's a person who kept preaching it and putting it in my head. Finally I started to believe it. I think I'm kind of fulfilling a lot of his dreams. It was kind of like he got drafted when I got drafted."

Smith and Hernandez graduated after the 1991 season, and Coleman was thrust into the leadership role among the receivers. He had a productive 1992, but struggled to catch the ball in the spring of 1993 and into the fall camp. A receiver who can't catch is not much of a help, and Coleman knew it.

"I was trying so hard because I felt like, 'This is it. If I don't produce this year, no more football for Andre,'" he said. "I thought I had screwed up my chances of playing in the pros."

Snyder also had put in Coleman as the primary kickoff and punt returner, adding more pressure.

"He went through some hard times not being as consistent as he would like," Snyder said. "Here was a guy who was struggling to catch the football and we've got him back returning punts."

Smith, who had returned as an undergraduate assistant coach, helped Coleman relax, and Coleman's season took off. After a horrendous first half of the first game in which he asked Snyder to take him out of the game, Coleman

broke through in the second half. He had a 31-yard reception that keyed the opening scoring drive. Then he broke a 74-yard punt return for a touchdown.

"Andre was a threat every time he had his hands on the ball," Snyder said.

He finished his senior year by leading the Big Eight in all-purpose yards, punt return yards and kickoff return yards, the first player ever to do that. His 72-yard kickoff return after Minnesota had taken a 25-24 lead, brought the Cats back and enabled them to claim their first non-conference road victory in 14 years. He was named second-team all-America by the NFL Draft Report and third-team by the AP.

Following his back-to-back MVP awards, Coleman attended the NFL Scouting Combine, where he turned in the fastest time (4.24) in the 40-yard dash of any of the athletes in attendance, including teammate Thomas Randolph, who has been classified as having world-class speed. "I've always had a knack for performing under pressure like that," he said. "It's kind of like the guy who has a knack for hitting a buzzer-beater. I've just been fortunate to have good games in every big game I've played in."

It couldn't have been scripted any better.

points to Nebraska, and that was a bad game. They play in the WAC and they're not known for defense. There are not that many WAC guys in the pros playing defense. I don't know where they built that up that it's going to be a 100-point game. Maybe our offense could score 50, but our defense wouldn't give up that many points, especially not in the air.

"We just knew. We just went in and proved it and talked after."

Wyoming never got untracked. Fullback Ryan Christopherson, who had gained more than 1,000 yards during the season, gained just 28 yards on 15 carries. The Cowboys even tried a trick play to throw off the Wildcats. Yarborough took a handoff on a reverse that hooked the secondary, leaving Mike Jones wide open at the goal line. But in one of the most amazing plays in a season of remarkable plays, Randolph raced from

Coleman's 4.24 40-yard-dash speed made it a sure thing that nobody would catch him on this punt-return TD.

behind the line of scrimmage to intercept a certain touchdown pass at the goal line.

"It was a busted play," Randolph said. "Jaime and I busted it; we were so hyped and ready to stop the play that when Yarborough went in reverse, I was behind the line of scrimmage, because I thought it was going to be a sweep. I looked and I couldn't believe it, Jones was running wide open.

"I saw Kenny running back, and I thought he might make it, but I thought I'd better try to get back there. I saw the ball go up in the air. I saw Kenny jump and it went over his head. I don't know what it is, but the last five steps were like snap, snap, snap. I saw the ball leave Yarborough's hand and the next thing I remember I was rolling on the ground, getting up and celebrating."

The crowd went crazy. The Wyoming sideline didn't.

"He couldn't believe it," Randolph continued. "I don't think they had seen the kind of speed we have in our secondary. Our whole team, speed wise, was outstanding, compared to theirs. But they didn't believe they were out of it, because the WAC is so explosive. They thought they could come back like they did on everybody else during the season. They came back on San Diego State and beat them and got a piece of the WAC championship. I don't think they were out of it until Andre ran that punt back right before halftime."

Meanwhile the Cats were starting to wrack up the points.

Following the interception, they drove 76 yards to a Tate Wright field goal and a 9-3 lead. Chad May followed that with a 2-yard quarterback sneak, capping another 76-yard drive, and the Cats were up by 13.

When Christopherson escaped a Jaime Mendez tackle and ran in from the 3, it brought the Cowboys within six at 16-10. But two Coleman TDs within 2:05 (sandwiched around halftime) broke open the game. With 1:07 left in the first half, Wyoming punted. Coleman took the ball on his own 32 and swept around the right end. He raced down the sideline with half the state of Wyoming chasing him. When May ran in the two-point conversion, the Cats held a 24-10 halftime lead.

The Cats got the opening kickoff in the second half. On the second play, May rolled right, waited, rolled some more, waited a bit longer, then ran to the sideline. Just before stepping out of bounds, he flipped the ball to Coleman who was open in the flat. Coleman headed toward the left corner of the end zone, outrunning all the pursuit with a 61-yard TD. Cats, 31-10. Game over.

"I think the punt return took a lot of steam out of them," Coleman said. "I think that's when (after the second touchdown) I knew it was over. It was going to be a fun game after that. It was going to be one of those games where everyone wants to get in and make a catch."

Snyder says he felt that play was as key as any play in the ballgame. "Maybe if there was a knock-out punch, that might have been it," he said. "I didn't accept it as a knock-out punch at the time, because we hadn't yet put two halves back-to-back in this entire season. This was a great opportunity to do it, and that's what we wanted to do."

The Cats really did, and Wyoming didn't like it. "They couldn't handle it at all," Randolph said. "They kept telling the refs, 'He's on me, he's touching me, he's pushing me.' And the ref was saying, 'This is football. He can touch you. He can push you. He can throw you down on the ground.'

"They weren't used to that style of play. And we said, 'Welcome to the Big Eight. That's how we play in the Big Eight. You (may) try to run around people. We're not going to let you run around us. We're not going to let you run a free path around the field. We're going to try to get our hands on you.' I think we just disrupted them, period."

Coleman's dashes illustrated the biggest difference between the two teams—team

Playing on grass for the first time in five years didn't slow down the Cats' offense, which scored the second-most points in school history.

163

Lockett's first Copper Bowl catch was another (ho-hum) spectacular touchdown catch.

speed. To a man, Wyoming gave credit to the Wildcats' advantage in team speed. "They are physical, with great foot speed," Christopherson said. "They were faster than on film," added defensive end Kurt Whitehead.

Coach Joe Tiller noted, "We were playing a talented team with more foot speed than we had. We thought part of the reason they looked fast on tape was because they'd played all year on Astroturf, and they'd slow down a little on grass. But a football team that can run has a chance any (week)."

Whitehead added one other difference. "They wanted it worse than we did," he said. "You could see a burning desire to win."

Every person who ever played any kind of neighborhood ball knew somebody like Kenny McEntyre. He was the kid you always picked first, no matter what sport you were playing that day, because he was that good.

"Kenny is a good, instinctive sandlot athlete," head coach Bill Snyder said. "I'm sure that when he was this tall, he was always out playing baseball or football in the sandlot, all those things you do when you're a young kid. He would rather go over and play basketball than go riding around in cars."

The competitive juices that led McEntyre to the sandlot also developed a great amount of confidence. He was always out to prove that he could do what others said he couldn't, whether it was playing a sport at the major college level or stopping the opponent's best receiver.

McEntyre started at cornerback, opposite Thomas Randolph, during his senior year. He lined up on the short side of the field, or on the middle receiver when the offense put three receivers

on a side. During the 1993 Copper Bowl, usually that meant going up against Ryan Yarborough, the NCAA career yardage leader.

"Their coaches thought Tom was going to be on him all the time, but we weren't going to change anything," he said. "If he goes on my side, I line up on him. I love the challenge."

Let the record show that Yarborough had 72 yards receiving on just eight catches. He came into the game averaging 137 yards per game.

McEntyre was a hot prospect coming out of Plano (Texas) East High School. He was all-district and all-metro as a defensive back. He was recruited by all the Southwest Conference schools, as well as Purdue and "a bunch of other Division I schools." But McEntyre didn't want to play football. He wanted to play basketball.

"I told people I wanted to play basketball since I was a little kid, all the way to the NBA," he said. So without any high school basketball experience, he arranged a tryout at Cloud County

Community College during spring break of his senior year, where he made the team. While at Cloud County, which is only about an hour from Manhattan, in Concordia, he attended most of K-State's home football games. When his two years were completed, he was ready to return to the football field, so he walked on to the program at K-State.

"All the coaches at my JuCo said, 'Don't do it.' They wanted me to continue to play basketball at a Division II school or football somewhere else. But I remembered a long time ago, they were getting beat like 74-10. (The K-State record for largest margin of defeat is 76-0, but that was against Oklahoma in 1942.) I was thinking, 'I've got to do it.'"

So McEntyre enrolled at K-State with three years of football eligibility remaining. "He just surfaced and said, 'Give me a chance,'" Snyder said. "We gave him a chance."

McEntyre took advantage, playing on special teams his first year, then backing up Randolph and Kitt Rawlings

Much of that flame could be traced to the fact that the Cats were in their first bowl game in 11 years, while the Cowboys were in their fourth in seven years. But it also goes back to Snyder's 14 goals.

"I spoke at the pep rally at the Copper Bowl, and it was incredible," said Brent Venables, who was an undergraduate assistant in 1993. "The entire trip was a huge, huge emotion for me. I just felt so much emotion for those guys, and envious of them as well. These guys knew how to win. That was the biggest difference. I was with the coaches in the booth and I could hear everything that was going on. Even when things weren't going well, the attitude was 'We will win this football game.'"

The Cats, with the victory firmly in hand, piled on the numbers. Following Coleman's second TD, May hit acrobatic freshman Kevin Lockett with a 30-yard lob on which Lockett out-leaped the defender. "We had the game under control and then when Kevin came up with that catch, it just put things out of reach," May said.

The Cowboys scored once more

at the corners during his junior season. Following his junior year on the football field, he suited up for coach Dana Altman's Wildcats on the basketball floor. He averaged two points per game with a season high of eight against Central Connecticut State. He was a part of the team that lost in the first round of the NCAA tournament to Tulane. When he stepped onto the field for the Copper Bowl, he became the first K-Stater to play in both the NCAA basketball tournament and a bowl game.

But the summer after the disappointing 5-6 season of his junior year, he dedicated himself to football. He knew his ticket to professional sports was in the NFL, not the NBA. He was part of a renewed dedication by many of the K-State footballers, who spent the summer in Manhattan in preparation for the 1993 season. He did not play basketball after his senior season because NFL scouts told him to avoid it to prevent possible injury.

McEntyre seems a good fit for the NFL. He "sees things taking place and consequently can get a jump on things," Snyder says. "I'm sure his basketball background has something to do with it. Again, it's just the fact that he has been around athletics all his life."

The NFL Draft Report called McEntyre "the best athlete in the Big Eight Conference" and the "most-underrated player in the country at his position." With Randolph and Jaime Mendez in the same defensive backfield, McEntyre got overlooked throughout most of his senior year. But the country finally found out what Snyder knew all along.

"Until late in the year, there was such acclaim for Jaime and Tommy that the others were overlooked," he said. "No one could conceive that there could be three high-profile secondary guys at one university, let alone it be Kansas State University. So Kenny kind of got shunned. Yet Kenny probably was as good an athlete back there as anybody that we ever had."

Even a Gatorade shower couldn't douse K-State's burning desire to win the school's first bowl game.

Leon Roberts (opposite page) took over for J.J. Smith in the second half and the Wildcats didn't miss a step.

after blocking a Chad Romano punt deep in KSU territory, but the Cats answered with two more scores. Leon Edwards, who had replaced Smith after Smith set the bowl record for rushing yards with 133, raced in from the 13. And McEntyre, the unsung cornerback in the K-State "Secondary to None," picked off John Gustin's pass and raced untouched 37 yards into the end zone.

"During the whole season, I was thinking 'I've got to get a touchdown,'" McEntyre said. "Tom and Jaime and I would talk about which one of us was going to get a touchdown. We all had interceptions, but that was the only interception returned for a touchdown all season.

"I knew he wasn't going to catch me. All of the fellows got on my back talking about how he was going to catch me, that he felt sorry for me or else he would have caught me. I said, 'He could have run 100 yards, he wasn't going to catch me.' That was a great feeling, getting a touchdown and winning."

It was the crowning achievement for a program that all too recently was simply, "the worst." Snyder takes great pride in being a part of something so special for so many people.

"It wasn't just the win, but it was how we won, and the whole setting for the 15,000 to 18,000 who were there. I've had thousands, either through correspondence or verbally, say that that was probably as monumental a period of time as they've had in their life. That's hard for me to imagine, but they are genuine and sincere about it. I'm awfully pleased that our players and coaches were able to help provide that kind of scenario for so many people. When you sit back and think about it, what an honor it is to have the opportunity to provide the most pleasant memories for an individual's life."

The trophy then got passed around. Mendez held the trophy in front of his face to hide the tears. "I cried after the game," Mendez said. "I went and hugged every senior on the team, hugged Coach Snyder, President Wefald and a couple of other people. I remember holding the trophy. Coach Snyder pointed to me and said, 'It makes me happy to see somebody who's been here with me since the beginning who knows what we went through and who is sad at the end of the game.' He knew why I was crying, because I was leaving my family for the past five years."

Coleman grabbed it, too, enjoying the fact that he could receive his offensive MVP award on the field in front of all his teammates and fans. "It was kind of icing on the cake to a great season," he said. "It was just a feeling that you can't imagine. If I had

While the Wildcats got to hoist a championship trophy for the first time, Coleman finally got his chance to claim an MVP award on the field.

accepted that award in Tokyo, I'm sure I wouldn't have felt close to the way I felt in Tucson."

Another goal had been reached.

A win. A win vs. a Division I-A team. A Big Eight win. A Big Eight road win. A winning season and an upper division finish. A win against a "Big Three" team. And finally a bowl win.

To many, it seemed like the pinnacle for Kansas State. But May summed up the attitude at Kansas State. "The atmosphere was nice," he said. "I was kind of used to it since I'm from California. It was kind of the same as it is out there. We had a good time while we were there. I know the team had a good time. I have nothing against the Copper Bowl, but I want to be somewhere else next year.

"Like Florida."

CONCLUSION
A TOTAL COMMITMENT

Where is Kansas State football headed? Will the success seen under Bill Snyder be repeated? Improved upon? What does the future hold?

The future is not about returning starters and letterwinners. Although Kansas State seems well stocked for the 1994 season, the future no longer means just the coming season. The future means five, 10 and 20 years down the line, and Kansas State seems equally prepared for that.

Bill Snyder is firmly entrenched as the head coach, now in his sixth year. He has all his own recruits playing his own system. And everyone involved in the football office on Kimball Avenue has committed to the same undying work ethic.

"Coach Snyder is the kind of person who never is satisfied," said linebacker Brooks Barta, who played for Snyder from 1989 to 1992. "Being a teacher and a coach now, that's the same type of thing that I try to portray to my players. He's not going to allow that program to go back down hill, and I don't think he'll allow people to be satisfied. They're bringing in the type of players they need to bring in to continue to succeed."

Once Snyder gets his type of player into the program, he has a chance to groom him. Snyder's offense is quite intricate, but once it is mastered, it is lethal. "Kansas State can compete with anybody," said Carl Straw, Snyder's quarterback the first two years. "You take a quarterback who has been in there three years and has learned that system and he literally can pick apart a defense piece by piece. And you have total con-

With Snyder on the sidelines, Kansas State should continue to charge up the national rankings.

trol over that, because Coach Snyder gives you that control."

The work ethic extends to the lower level of the Vanier Football Complex and the weight room. "The NCAA allows us eight hours per week during the off-season. That's two hours a day, four days a week," strength and conditioning coach Rod Cole said. "We use every minute of that. We also have developed an attitude where our guys will come in and do the extra work. I think that's very important. Over the last three years, we've gotten to where we average more than 50 guys who stay here during the summer. This year we have 64. They hold one another accountable, they push each other.

"We are developing the power to play football. We do a lot of the Olympic lifts – cleans, snatches, cleans and jerks – that are quick lifts that develop attributes that carry over to football."

Another reason the Cats seem destined to stay at or above their current level is the continued support from the same administration that allowed Snyder's program to get past ground zero. "K-State has made a commitment, from the president on down, that football will be strong," said Erick Harper, who was a senior in Snyder's first year and now heads the Golden Cats, a group of former Wildcats football players who raise money for football. "They will not settle for second-rate."

Combine solid returning athletes, hard work, and a supportive administration, and add the quality of recruits that success brings, and it may be time to change the goals. When Snyder took over in December of 1988, he said his goal was to have each of his players improve every day, as a player, a person and a student. If each player on the team improved, logic had it that the team would be successful. Coming off a 9-2-1 season and a Copper Bowl victory, how had those goals changed? Not one iota.

"It's kind of like building a quality house," Snyder said. "If you have a certain material that you use that is better than another material, why would you change and go

With the new indoor facility, the Cats should have no trouble focusing... on the next opponent or the long-term goals of the program.

back and do it a different way? If we've made progress in our program, then why would we want to try to reinvent the wheel? Why would we want to do it differently?

"If the team goals were important in developing this program to whatever level it might be at right now, if they allowed us to have some success, and that's the premise that they did, then why change the direction that we've taken to get there?"

The end result may be different. Instead of trying to win *a* game, as was the result in 1989, instead of trying to win in the Big Eight, on the road and against a nationally ranked opponent, as happened in the subsequent years, continued success will mean heretofore unthinkable milestones.

Yet, not one step can be skipped.

"Every individual in this world sets goals every single day," Snyder said. "But we forget some of the things that go in the middle. The middle phase of it is having a good

solid plan about how you're going to get there and taking it step by step. That's kind of what the program is doing.

"We could talk about setting goals from point A to a national championship, but it's the stuff in the middle that makes the difference. That's what our goals are. Our goals are that plan. We want to achieve each one of those, step by step."

Steve Miller, the former KSU athletic director who hired Snyder and who began his career in athletics as a track coach, agrees.

"It's similar to what I've always told athletes who are getting ready to leave college and are trying to make a lot of money in sports," he said. "Just keep competing well, jumping far, throwing far and running fast and you'll make money. You can't think about making money first. Bill is right. You do the best job that you can and everything else takes care of itself."

Certainly the Wildcats are better prepared to meet some of those challenges than they were in 1989. Despite losing five players to the NFL following the 1993 season and graduating 11 starters, including three offensive linemen and the entire secondary, there's plenty of talent left behind. Big Eight Newcomers of the Year on offense (quarterback Chad May) and defense (linebacker Percell Gaskins) return to highlight the experience. The depth is there too.

"We're very confident in what they (the replacements) will be able to do and that they'll be able to win for us," said Bobby Stoops, who, as co-defensive coordinator and secondary coach, has the chore of replacing a secondary that sent three of the four starters to the pros. "It doesn't frighten me at all, losing those guys. It's time for them to leave. They were tired of listening to me and I was tired of talking to them. We're very close and we have great respect for each other, but it's another guy's time now."

May and Snyder have one more season to confer, which will strengthen the foundation of winning.

"I feel great about the guys coming in. They've seen how it's done."

Repeating the nine wins will be no easy task. The Wildcats will sneak up on no one in 1994. They have to travel to Colorado, Oklahoma and Kansas, places in which they have not won since 1973, 1970 and 1969, respectively. But nobody is doubting the Cats' chances. "No matter if you're a great team or not, nine wins is difficult," co-defensive coordinator Jim Leavitt said. "But we have the talent to do anything."

That's the spoken plan of many of the players. Chad May says he's ready to go. Thomas Randolph, who will be toiling in the secondary of the New York Giants in 1994, says, "I will be there at the Orange Bowl." And if the Giants are preparing for the NFL playoffs? "I've got to get down there," he said with a gleam in his eye. "I've got to go see my boys in the Orange Bowl."

Doug Looney, who made few friends in Manhattan when he dubbed Kansas State "Futility U." in a 1989 *Sports Illustrated* article, says the Cats have achieved enough that they no longer will be allowed to be mediocre. "They've raised the fans' expectations," he said.

The Wildcats have established themselves as a team that draws well at a bowl game, a fact that should not elude bowl officials.

But not any higher than their own. "We've had a taste of winning nine games and a bowl game," Stoops said. "Our guys are hungry for it now. What's great is nine (wins) isn't enough. You'd think maybe a program like ours would be satisfied, but it's made our players that much more hungry to get a championship."

Snyder will head into the 1994 season in a new situation. None of the players on the roster ever have been part of a K-State team with a record worse than 5-6, even as redshirts. So while they have had the benefit of experiencing winning, they won't be motivated by how bad 1-10 feels.

"There's guys who have gotten in on the benefits and haven't quite learned what it took in order to get here," he said. "That's a real important part of (keeping our goals consistent). If we change what we are doing, then these guys would never be attuned to what it really has taken to get where we are and why that all took place."

That's where he is relying on the departed veterans. "I have a great appreciation for the youngsters in our program who have finished their eligibility here who are still taking the leadership responsibility in being able to confront those who are still in the program," he continued. "They say, 'You can't let down; you can't come in here doing what you're doing right now and have the kind of success that you want to have.' They're willing to hold these young guys accountable. That's the thing that I've shared with our players from day one is that a degree and an end to your eligibility doesn't mean that you're no longer a complete, total,

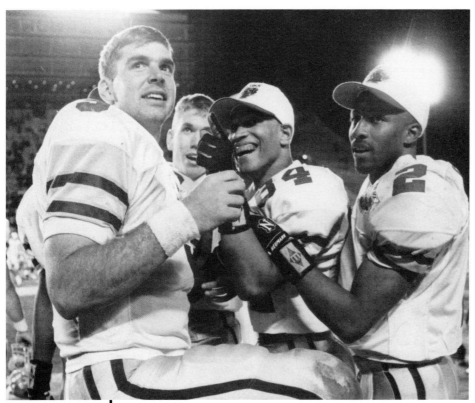

Now that the Cats have tasted a bowl victory, the goal is to celebrate a victory in the Orange Bowl as the Big Eight champions.

embraced member of this program."

It's players like Quentin Neujahr, who came to K-State because it was the only Division I-A school to offer him a scholarship and left as a second-team all-America with a free-agent shot at the NFL. He still can be found in the weight room, exhorting the younger players. "We're not going to get outworked," he says. "I honestly believe that Kansas State is here to stay. This isn't a shot in the dark. This isn't a one-night stand."

Snyder believes the upcoming season is one of the most important ever. Support cannot die, either philosophical, financial or fanatical. "There still is a direction to go," he said. "It's important that it's approached with the same diligence that it was five years ago. Because you can go in other directions. You've seen Kansas State on a couple of occasions before at least approach a level of respectability and then die off again. So you don't want history to repeat itself in this particular situation. It's going to require so many things.

"We can't assume that we have arrived to a point where we don't have to be as financially well supported. Our constituency has to continue to grow. There's steps that everybody still can take, and need to take, in order for us to continue to make progress here."

That support that Snyder is requesting is starting to take off *outside* the state of Kansas.

"All of a sudden there is so much inquiry," said Frank Hernandez, who played for Snyder from 1989 through 1991 and now is the receivers coach at Mission (Texas) High School. "The players ask, 'When is Kansas State going to send me a letter?' Or 'When is K-State going to be on TV?' Or 'What is K-State ranked?'

"I hear the general questions you hear about other Top 20 programs."

Where is this program headed? The same place it was headed in 1989.

Up.

"Kansas State football is here," said Brent Venables, a two-year player at linebacker for Snyder in 1991 and 1992. "It's finally here. And it's not going back down. Coach Snyder, his football staff and those players put it all together."

The final chapter just is not yet written...